Sleeping Like a Baby

Sleeping Like a Baby

A Sensitive and Sensible Approach to Solving
Your Child's Sleep Problems

Avi Sadeh

Yale University Press New Haven and London

Designed by Sonia Shannon
Set in Cochin type by Binghamton Valley Composition.
Printed in the United States of America.

Library of Congress Cataloging-in-Publication Data
Sadeh, Avi, 1957–
[Lishon kemo tinoòk. English]
Sleeping like a baby : a sensitive and sensible approach to solving your child's
sleep problems / Avi Sadeh.
p. cm.
Includes bibliographical references and index.
ISBN 0-300-08824-8
1. Infants — Sleep. 2. Sleep disorders in children. 3. Parent and infant. I. Title.
BF720.S3313 2001
649'.4—dc21 00-011100

A catalogue record for this book is available from the British Library.

The paper in this book meets the guidelines for permanence and durability
of the Committee on Production Guidelines for Book Longevity of the
Council on Library Resources.

10 9 8 7 6 5 4 3 2 1

This book is dedicated to the memory of my mother, Pnina,
who did not live to see my children, awake or asleep,
and to my father, David Hirschfeld,
a flowing brook of tenderness, peacefulness, and love.

Contents

Contents

Contents

Preface

The expression "sleeping like an angel" is usually reserved for babies. A sleeping baby is perceived by many as angelic, the essence of purity. The smile that initially appears during sleep adds a magical aura. On the other hand, a baby who refuses to sleep is perceived as a terrible nightmare, threatening family harmony and breeding jealousy of all those parents of "real angels." Luckily, the newborn doesn't come home from the hospital with a money-back guarantee.

What is the importance of sleep to a baby? What makes sleeping babies laugh and what frightens them? How is sleep related to development? How do babies in different cultures sleep? How is a baby's sleep influenced by his relationship to his parents, and how does the baby's sleep influence them? What causes "crib death"? How can we distinguish between "little angels" and "little devils" at night? What can parents do to be able to report in the morning, "Our baby slept through the night"? In what strange ways do babies calm themselves down? And what is different in the sleep of premature babies? In this book I shall attempt to answer these and other questions.

The book is presented from a personal point of view and is based on years of research and clinical work with sleep-deprived parents and their "night-shift" babies. It is meant primarily for parents who want to learn what happens to them and to their own private angel at night. The book also makes use of documented scientific research and should be valuable to professionals who treat children and their families, and to scientists interested in the subject.

I hope you enjoy reading this book — ideally, during a pleasant afternoon while your child is busy playing by your side, or, failing that, in the middle of the night with your child crying desperately in the next room, trying to convince you that babies also have a right to an active night life.

Acknowledgments

First, I would like to thank Peretz Lavie for introducing me to the magical world of sleep, and for his friendship and support over the years. Thanks to Miriam Ben Aharon for her many years of supervision and encouragement in working with babies and their parents. Many thanks to Mary Carskadon, Thomas Anders, and Christine Acebo for providing excellent opportunities to learn about infants' and children's sleep.

Thanks to Reut Gruber for her editing and her contribution of brilliant ideas. Thanks to Ornit Arbel and to Nissim and Jennifer Yehezkel for all their help and wonderful support.

Thanks to Yael for her friendship and love, day and night. A warm hug to Adi, Gil, and Roni, who taught me, night after night, about children's sleep.

Finally, many thanks to the hundreds of parents and babies who trusted me and participated in my research studies or who helped me in solving their sleep problems.

I
Sleep and Development

1

"Why do we sleep?"

The Significance and Role of Sleep

The newborn, in the first days of life, spends approximately two-thirds of each twenty-four-hour period asleep. Over the course of a lifetime, the length of sleep decreases until old age, when humans spend only about a quarter of a twenty-four-hour period asleep. Over the course of our lifetime we spend about one-third of our time sleeping.

There are those who view sleep as a waste of time and those who view it as an unfettered pleasure. Some sleep many hours, and others, few. There are those who awake early and go to sleep early and others who are night owls. It doesn't matter to which camp we belong — sleep is an integral part of our lives.

It often seems that the question of why we sleep is utterly unnecessary, for we all know what happens when we try or are forced to shorten or refrain from sleeping for one reason or another. The primary and strongest expression of lack of sleep is a growing desire to sleep, which becomes increasingly hard to fight. If we refuse to respond to the subtle signals that it's time to sleep, the physiologic need can overrule our resistance. The need to sleep is so strong that sleep deprivation is often considered to be the most excruciating form of torture. Indeed, many parents begin to relate to their sleepless baby as an Inquisitor who intentionally prevents them from sleeping in order to make them suffer.

But the irresistability of sleep doesn't explain its role. Many years of research in the field of sleep and the ramifications of sleep deprivation have left many questions unanswered. We know that animals that are deprived of sleep for an extended period of time become exhausted and die. We know that sleeplessness gradually damages our subtler mental functions of attention and concentration, and then wider functions of information processing, learning, and memory. We know that in cases of continued sleep deprivation the immune system's ability to respond weakens and physical health is damaged. On the basis of hundreds of studies we can conclude that sleep is a physiologic need analogous to the need for nutritious food. Just as one can go on a diet and control, to some extent, the amount of food ingested, it is possible to change sleep patterns to a certain degree. But severe sleep restriction, like a severe diet, will lead to significant functional damage.

All animals known to us must sleep, or at least spend some of their time in what resembles a state of rest or sleep. Modern research has revealed essential differences in the sleep of various animals and has shed light on brain activity during sleep. Many species of bat, for example, sleep nineteen hours out of twenty-four, as opposed to the giraffe, which sleeps a mere two hours per day. Dolphins sleep in a surprisingly clever way. At any given time, only one hemisphere of the animal's brain is asleep, while the other half is awake. In this way, a certain level of alertness and attention to the environment is always maintained, even during sleep.

The sleep pattern of dolphins illustrates that sleep is adapted to both the physiologic and the environmental needs of an animal. Sleep is precarious for helpless animals who are unable to hide or protect themselves. They live in fear of unpredicted predators. Nonetheless, field studies reveal that some sleeping animals succeed in escaping from seemingly imminent destruction by using senses that remain active. Certain characteristics of sleep, such as the amount of dream-sleep (a dangerous state for an animal), change fundamentally when a high danger of predation exists.

The fact that babies need so much sleep is evidence, perhaps, that they have a limited ability to be awake, or that they have heightened needs for rest and recuperation from wakefulness. Many theories have been proposed to explain the different sleep needs among diverse animals over the course of development. For instance, research on animals provides evidence that an animal's physical size is directly related to the amount of time it spends sleeping. As the animal's physical size increases, its need for sleep decreases. In addition, animals that sleep less live longer. Finally, some theories relate amount of sleep to the body's hormonal status, to the maintenance of body temperature, to energy conservation, and so on. Without attempting to explain these complex theories, we can say that when a baby sleeps, she disconnects, to a certain extent, from the environment that bombards her with stimuli. She sinks into a state that resembles, in many ways, her former fetal state. This protected state simultaneously allows physical rest and brain activity that aids in brain maturation and develops functions of processing and storing information received during wakefulness and recorded in memory.

We might fancifully speculate that evolution was considerate of parents: it treats them to a grace period so that they can gradually get used to their baby. The baby's abundant sleep in the first months gives parents some free time in which to recuperate from the demanding and all-encompassing job of caring for baby.

2

"What's so interesting about a sleeping baby?"

What Sleep Is and How We Can Peek into a Child's "Night Life"

What is simpler than looking at a sleeping baby? Parents do so day and night, to ensure that baby is well, or purely for the pleasure of it. Every experienced parent can report interesting impressions of baby's sleep: "He doesn't stop moving," "She smiles so that you can see the whites of her gums," "She starts the night on one side of the crib and ends up on the other side," "He snores louder than his father," and so on.

When scientists look at sleeping babies, they do so to understand normal child development and early childhood sleep disturbances. In the first year of life, the baby is limited in her ability to demonstrate her mental abilities and talents. Hence researchers need sophisticated research methods in order to ascertain this information. Using these methods, we can witness more and more abilities of young babies that we knew nothing about in the past. The perceptual and intellectual abilities of the baby, for example, were discovered via such methods. These abilities exist from the first few weeks of life and, among other things, enable the baby to relate to one significant figure who cares for her, usually her mother.

Many studies show that the human baby is visually perceptive and selective. The baby focuses on characteristics of stimuli that resemble human facial characteristics more than those that do not. It has also been found that attention to sounds is selective and that babies only days old prefer human voices to other sounds. These preferences, which exist for other sensory systems as well, show that the baby is "programmed" to home in on human contact. A baby's sleep-wake patterns result from one of his world's most complex systems, which can be studied in a simple and direct fashion from the baby's first few days of life. As with patterns of eating, attention, social behavior, and movement, sleep patterns are an important sign of nervous system maturation and of the child's behavioral organization. The study of sleep in childhood facilitates our understanding of the importance of sleep in the developmental process and the relation between sleep-wake patterns and various other functional systems. Sleep patterns are influenced by neural and bodily systems, by environmental stimuli, and by family patterns. They offer a vast field for the study of the relations among all these complex systems. As a result, the study of sleep is a major subject in interdisciplinary research, involving biologists, physiologists, pediatricians, neurologists, heart and lung specialists, digestive system specialists, and developmental and clinical psychologists.

One of the central fields for understanding sleep in childhood is research that investigates the sources and reasons for common sleep disturbances. Approximately 20 to 30 percent of all babies and their parents cope with sleep disturbances, especially difficulties falling asleep or frequent and lengthy awakenings during the night. In order to assess sleep disturbances and to treat them, we must study and understand normal developmental processes. This understanding of sleep helps us answer basic questions related to sleep disturbances: What is abnormal, and at what age? Are sleep problems solved by the passing of time? Is treatment intervention necessary? Is treating sleep problems effective, and which treatments are most appropriate and effective?

In a typical discussion parents talk about when the baby falls asleep, when she awakens, when she naps, and how she refuses to sleep at night. The most basic common discrimination in these discussions is between sleep and wakefulness. Parents usually relate to the length and frequency of each condition over a twenty-four-hour period. However, are these two conditions all-inclusive?

The breakthrough that made the study of sleep a unique scientific field was also a result of looking at sleeping babies. In the early 1950s Eugene Asrinsky, a young student who worked with a professor of philosophy named Nathaniel Kleitman, observed the appearance of rapid eye movements that could be easily identified even though the babies' eyes were shut. Asrinsky and Kleitman found that while a baby sleeps, cycles of two distinct patterns alternate over the course of a night: quiet sleep, with steady and deep breathing and relatively no body movements, and "active" sleep, characterized by rapid eye movements, rapid body movements, and twitches, mostly of the fingers, toes, and face muscles.

This discovery of active sleep — also called stormy sleep or dream sleep or REM sleep, for "rapid eye movements" — as opposed to quiet or non-REM sleep, was a breakthrough in the understanding that sleep is not a homogeneous process which takes place over the course of a night. Rather, the process comprises a series of distinct physiological states. When adult REM sleep was studied in the laboratory, people who were awakened from this state of sleep tended to remember dreams and to report them (hence the term "dream sleep"). It became clear that the activities of both brain and body in this type of sleep physiologically more closely resemble wakeful activity than quiet wakefulness or quiet sleep.

Parents of babies can easily discern dream sleep, which frequently is evidenced immediately after the baby falls asleep. Her eyes dart about, her fingers or toes twitch rapidly or suddenly, and short smiles, grimaces, or other distortions appear on her face. Looking at a baby and the changes in the stages of sleep leads us to the more important aspect of sleep — the roles of internal biological clocks in the baby's brain. Here is where the appearance of each stage of sleep is determined, timed according to when the baby will feel tired and will be ready to sleep, as well as when he will awaken and feel alert.

Biological Clocks and Sleep Cycles

Many of our bodily functions have cycles or rhythms, according to which certain events recur. When we talk about a biological clock, we are actually speaking of these rhythms.

The term *biological clock* is, in fact, deceptive. Imagine a clock shop in which each clock was set at a different time, ticked at a different pace, and chimed or buzzed or cuckooed at a different interval. This is a fair analogy to our "biological clocks": our bodies contain many unsynchronized clocks that influence many events and are in turn influenced by them. Perhaps the best known are the sleep-wake clock, which completes a cycle approximately every twenty-four hours, and a woman's ovulation, which completes its cycle in approximately one month. It is important to recognize that these clocks are interrelated. Each is regulated by environmental stimulation, and the concurrent cycles are part of that environment. The day-night cycle, which is expressed in cycles of light and darkness, passes on information about the seasons of the year, according to the length of the day.

Two basic rhythms are related to sleep. The first is the sleep-wake cycle, which in an adult is a circadian rhythm — that is, approximately twenty-four hours. The span between one event of sleep and the next event of sleep is, more or less, twenty-four hours, and the events of waking from sleep are similarly spaced.

The second important rhythm in sleep is the ultradian rhythm between the various stages of sleep — between active sleep and quiet sleep, for example. This rhythm, which changes over the course of the night, is, on average, sixty minutes among babies and about ninety minutes among older children and adults.

Different Methods for Examining a Baby's Sleep

In order to understand how a baby's sleep is examined and measured, we must establish how we define sleep and what distinguishes sleep from different wakeful states. These definitions remain scientifically controversial. One widely accepted definition describes sleep as a state in which three conditions exist: (1) a significant drop in alertness and response to environmental stimuli; (2) a significant drop in the level of body activity; (3) the partial or absolute disappearance of rational thought processes and of consciousness. But contrary to the intuitive notion that sleep entails a cessation of response to the environment, research has shown that we are responsive to the environment even in sleep. Ultimately, the definition of sleep is largely dependent upon the instrument that is used to examine it.

The Method of Direct Observation

It is possible to study babies' sleep simply by observing it, as many parents do. Indeed, many studies were based on direct observation of a sleeping baby. These studies found that not only does a baby sleep less as he grows older, but he spends relatively less time in active sleep and more in quiet and deeper sleep. The observations, made in the baby's natural setting (usually the crib), allowed documentation of sleep in natural conditions. Because direct observations require great effort, they are usually limited to a few hours over the course of a twenty-four-hour period.

Examining Sleep in the Laboratory

The most detailed physiological data about what happens during sleep are gathered in the laboratory. In an examination of this nature, the child or baby is brought to the sleep laboratory in the evening. Electrodes are attached to specific areas on the body and especially on the head, and the subject sleeps in a secluded room. Young children usually have a parent in the room in order to ease the stress that may be fostered by the conditions of the examination. Sometimes when the child resists having electrodes attached to his head, they are connected after he falls asleep. The nighttime examination is relatively uneventful for most babies, but some exhibit a stress reaction sufficient to compromise the quality of the examination (as well as the quality of the baby's sleep). Because the examination is expensive, it is usually conducted for only

Direct Observations of Infant Sleep-Wake States

The following states are directly observable by parents themselves. Parents who watch their baby at length, at different times of the day, will be able to distinguish these different stages:

Fussy-crying The baby is physically active, his eyes are open or closed, and he often cries loudly.

Alert The baby is physically active, her eyes are open, and her glance is active and alert. The baby doesn't cry.

Drowsy The baby is alternately physically active or quiet. Her eyes have a glassy, unfocused expression and open and close slowly.

Active sleep The baby sleeps, displaying rapid eye movements and twitches in the fingers, toes, and face (smiles and other facial expressions). Breathing is irregular.

Quiet sleep The baby sleeps quietly. His eyes are closed, with no rapid eye movements. Movements are subdued, though sucking or chewing activity may take place. Breathing is regular.

Transitional sleep It is difficult to determine whether the baby is in active or quiet sleep.

one night, and therefore the information gleaned from it is limited because great changes can occur in a child's sleep from one night to another.

Home Videotaping

Tracking by videotaping, which documents the baby's sleep and parental intervention, is an additional type of

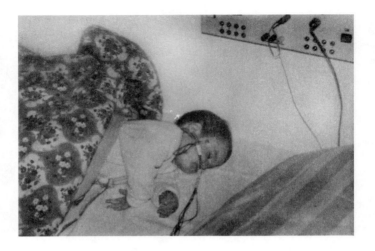

1

A baby sleeping in a sleep laboratory with electrodes attached.

sleep examination. The video camera is put above the baby's crib, and her state, movements, and behavior can be filmed. Usually, the recording is based on time-lapse video that condenses the night into one to two hours of recordings. The video also shows parental intervention because it is done in the baby's natural conditions. It supplies much information about his sleep, with minimal disturbance to the family.

The Pressure-Sensitive Mattress

This recording procedure employs a mattress that is sensitive to pressure and movements. The baby's movements and his breathing patterns are recorded, and this information reveals the child's sleep characteristics. This procedure, too, allows detailed documentation of sleep characteristics in the baby's natural environment.

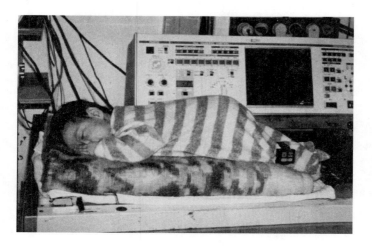

2

A baby sleeping with a sleep watch attached to her ankle.

The "Sleep Watch"

One of the most popular methods of sleep research in recent years is the use of an actigraph, or "sleep watch." This device, which resembles a digital wristwatch, is strapped on the baby's wrist or ankle. The sleep watch records the baby's bodily movements nightly over the course of weeks. From the activity patterns, the baby's sleep-wake patterns can be determined with great precision. Times of falling asleep and awakening can be determined, as well as the times the baby is in quiet, deep sleep or in active (dream) sleep. Night wakings and their frequency can be detected, and often the existence of sleep disturbances with physiological sources is revealed.

3

A toddler playing, with the sleep watch attached.

Questionnaires and a Baby's Sleep Diary

With or without sophisticated techniques of recording sleep, parents are the most important source of information about the baby's sleep-wake patterns and related behaviors. In order to produce this information in the most precise manner, parents are asked to complete a sleep diary for the baby in which they describe his sleep-wake patterns and relevant information (see Appendix 1). Related information includes the parent-infant interactions at bedtime and during the nights when the baby wakes up.

Much of the information gathered about infant sleep is consistent across different measurement methods. However, important discrepancies are frequently evident and provide valuable information. For instance, parents are very accurate reporters of their child's sleep-wake schedule, but their knowledge of the child's sleep *quality* is lim-

Sleep and a Child's "Night Life"

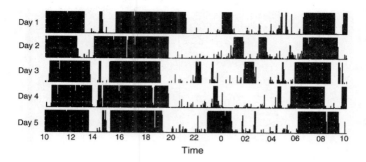

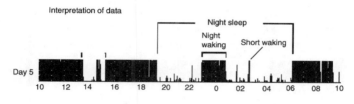

4

A sample record of a year-old baby's sleep-wake patterns over the course of five consecutive twenty-four-hour periods. The detailed explanation in the lower frame represents the last night of the diagram. The baby's activity level each minute is recorded. The "black" areas are those of great activity, usually identified as wakefulness. The quiet areas with low levels of activity are usually identified as quiet or active sleep.

ited. Parents are aware of night wakings only if the child makes some signal or demands their attention. Often infants can stay awake for prolonged periods during the night (as documented by video recordings or the sleep watch) without their parents becoming involved or being aware of this fact. In other situations, infants can have a fragmented or disturbed sleep because of various physiological reasons, but they do not reach full awakening and do not require intervention. In such cases, unless a complementary objective sleep assessment method is used, the active night life of the baby remains obscure.

3

"She sleeps when she feels like it, two hours here, two hours there"

The Formation of Sleep Patterns

An impressive developmental process that can be directly observed by parents is related to changes in their baby's sleep-wake patterns. In the baby's first months, her parents' lives (in some families, mainly her mother's life) revolve around her sleeping and waking schedule. Some babies have a relatively predictable and orderly schedule from day one. Others present a real challenge to their parents' ability to predict when they will sleep at length and when they will awaken and demand care.

The Newborn's Sleep

Until the 1940s most people believed that babies spend almost all their time sleeping during their first few days of life. There were even professional statements that newborns and young babies *must* sleep almost all the time (twenty to twenty-two hours per day) in order to grow. These common fallacies were based on beliefs and general impressions, not on methodical examination of the sleeping and waking

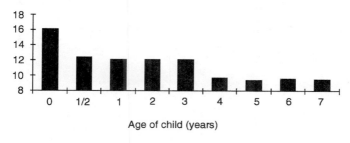

Amount of sleep in a 24-hour period

5

Sleep across development.

states of babies. Such an impressionistic approach might not distinguish, for example, between a sleeping baby and one who was wakeful yet quiet and comfortable in the bassinet. Not until 1958 were studies undertaken that included prolonged, continuous observations of babies. These studies showed that newborns actively sleep on average only two-thirds of a twenty-four-hour period. Many subsequent studies confirmed this finding and documented that substantial differences exist in the amount of time that individual babies sleep, and that these differences exist from the first days of life.

In the largest recent study of its kind, we recently examined (in cooperation with Dr. Betty Vohr and Irving Dark, of Mothers and Infants Hospital in Providence, Rhode Island) sleep-wake patterns of 220 babies during their first or second day of life in the newborn nursery. The examination was conducted by recording activity patterns with sleep watches for twenty-four consecutive hours. Our results confirmed earlier findings that newborns sleep an average of two-thirds of the time. Striking differences, however, were found between individual babies. Some babies slept as little as nine hours per day, and

Percent of infants

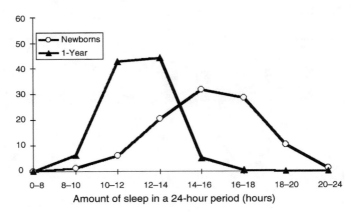

6

Individual and age group differences in sleep time.

others slept almost twenty-one hours. The significance of these large individual differences over the course of the first few days of life is not yet clear. The next stages of the study will perhaps shed light on the developmental ramifications of these differences.

Another popular opinion of days gone by was that in the first few months of life, sleep is randomly distributed over each twenty-four-hour period, with no preference for nighttime hours. This belief also was disproved when babies were carefully observed, though the view remained widely held in the professional literature. In 1945 scientists reported greater nighttime sleep and longer intervals between the baby's feedings on demand at night (3.61 hours) than during the day (2.86 hours).

In our Rhode Island study, we divided a twenty-four-hour period into two identical periods of day (from 7 A.M. to 7 P.M.) and night (from 7 P.M. to 7 A.M. the following day). We found that the newborns spent significantly more

The Formation of Sleep Patterns

Percent of children sleeping at each hour of the day

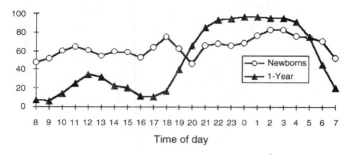

7

Distribution of sleep across the day.

time in sleep at night than during the day. Other scientists who reported similar findings have concluded that their results indicate that newborns are born with a biological clock that favors nighttime sleep. We must remember, however, that newborns in a hospital nursery are exposed to many environmental conditions that influence them and their sleep cycles. It is quieter at night and in some nurseries it is darker than during the daytime. Fewer treatments and examinations are administered at night. For all these reasons, it is probably easier for babies to sleep at night than during the day. At this point, however, we do not know whether an inborn preference exists, whether sleep becomes night-timed in response to the environment over the course of the first months, or even whether maternal hormones and activities begin this training before birth.

Figure 8 illustrates twenty-four-hour activity recordings of nine babies. We can see that the newborn's sleep is distributed over the course of a twenty-four-hour period in four to six sleep episodes that last from three to five hours each and are separated by relatively brief periods of wakefulness. One of the important activities dur-

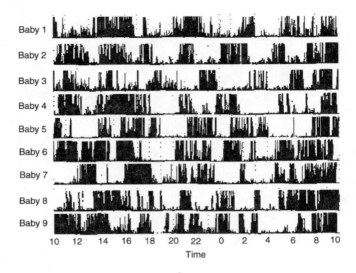

8

Sleep and activity data of nine babies across the day: raw data
derived from the sleep watch.

ing these waking episodes is, of course, food ingestion.
The newborn awakens frequently due to growing hunger
and falls asleep again after a satisfying meal. In the first
months, the baby enjoys Mom's relatively generous tolerance for and attention to his nighttime feeding needs.
This tolerance stems from both the parental expectation
of baby's period of adaptation (including his nocturnal
nutritional needs) and from the fact that baby also sleeps
at length during the day. Gradually, with baby's development, a clear parental expectation emerges that baby
will give up nighttime meals and "parties" and will begin
to sleep straight through the night.

Figure 8 also shows that some babies spend a significant amount of their time in very quiet sleep (with almost
no body movements) while others spend most of their
time in very active sleep (with almost incessant body

movements). In addition to day-night sleep-wake cycles, some scientists have examined whether shorter cycles of alternating sleep stages within a sleep episode (cycles between "quiet" and "active" sleep or "dream" and "non-dream" sleep) exist among newborns. The answer to this question varies from study to study, probably because of differences in research and statistical methods. Some studies have found no predictable and regular sleep cycles. Others have found predictable cycles of quiet and active sleep in newborns a day or two old. The duration of a quiet-active sleep cycle is, on average, sixty minutes. Large individual differences exist, however, between babies in this sleep characteristic.

This is an appropriate place to ask what variables influence or explain these significant individual differences between babies in sleep-wake characteristics.

Factors That Influence the Newborn's Sleep

The newborn has just gone through the process of birth, a difficult experience demanding transition and adaptation as he moves from a fetal environment to an external world that requires independent functioning. As we have seen, he sleeps long hours during the first few days of life, though significant differences exist both in the amount that individual newborns sleep and in the quality of their sleep. Some of these differences appear to be inherent and are manifested, for example, in the huge differences seen in the sleep-wake patterns of newborns during their first days of life. Before any other external factors can have an impact we see babies who sleep twenty hours a day and babies who sleep only eight. Some babies sleep continuously for a period of five hours whereas others are unable to sleep for more than an hour at a time. These inherent tendencies are often reflected in parents' descriptions of babies who slept throughout the night from the beginning and those who report never having an uninterrupted night of sleep from the time their baby was born. These inherent differences and their possible genetic source have never been systematically investigated and are not fully understood.

Environmental influences on infant sleep have been documented in many studies. Identified factors include maternal characteristics like personality, employment status, and education. A depressed, anxious, or unemployed mother, for example, is more likely to have a baby with a sleep problem. Parental beliefs, behaviors, and child-rearing practices have been found to be closely associated with infant sleep; parents who are more actively involved in their infant's process of falling asleep are more likely to have a baby with a sleep problem. The child's sleeping arrangements — sleeping with parents, feeding style, type of nutrition, lighting conditions, and many other environmental factors — may also have an impact on the baby's sleep patterns.

The researcher Maureen Kaffa examined whether there is a difference between the sleep of newborns who sleep in the same rooms with their mothers (rooming in) in the hospital after birth and of those who sleep only in a communal nursery. Sleep patterns were examined over the course of two days, using special equipment that was connected to the baby's bassinet. The results showed that newborns who roomed in with their mothers spent less time crying and more time sleeping quietly than newborns who slept in the nursery. The babies who roomed in also received more touch and attention from their mothers than those who slept in the nursery. In addition, mothers' caretaking was more appropriately timed for rooming-in babies vis-à-vis the babies' sleep-wake states. Mothers could wait until babies were awake to interact with them. The study also revealed significant differences in exposure to noise and light in the babies' sleep environments. In the mother's room, noise and light levels may have been more appropriate for the baby's sleep needs. Kaffa concluded that rooming in is preferable to other alternatives.

Another group of scientists in Montreal examined to what extent sleep patterns of newborns were influenced by an additional feeding administered three hours after their regular meal. Some of the babies were given a nutritional supplement, and others were given an identical amount of water. Their results showed that as the next feeding time approached, the babies who received water cried more and slept less than the babies who had received additional food. The authors concluded that sleep is directly influenced by nutritional status. They claimed that their study may support the traditional length of time between a newborn's meals, four hours.

In our study in the United States, we found two important variables that significantly influenced sleep patterns of newborns. A baby who was her mother's first child tended to sleep less quietly and peacefully than babies with older siblings. In addition, babies who were born by Cesarean section spent more time in active sleep, compared with newborns who were born in regular births. These findings suggest that birth factors may temporarily influence newborns' sleep in a way that resembles the stress response found in other studies (increased active sleep).

It is also interesting to note that, as many studies have shown, newborns who are born at the end of a full-term pregnancy exhibit more mature sleep patterns — in particular, more time spent in quiet sleep — than babies born prematurely, after a pregnancy that lasts thirty-six weeks or less. On the other hand, when babies are compared based on date of conception, differences disappear in most of the studies. Thus the systems responsible for sleep-wake patterns can mature both inside and outside of the womb. Babies who spend nine months in the uterus show more mature sleep patterns at birth, and babies born prematurely continue the maturation process after they are born. No special problems in sleep development occur in children who are born prematurely as long as there are no other complications related to premature birth.

We now know which factors influence the newborn's sleep, but are these sleep-wake differences really important? Do the newborn's sleep patterns have any significance or do they represent a temporary reaction to the traumatic passage to an extrauterine environment? Studies that have examined these questions suggest that sleep patterns of the newborn contain information that can predict aspects of the child's later development and can in some cases even point to the possibility of certain nervous-system anomalies.

In the first months of life, two developmental processes occur quickly at the same time: the total amount of sleep in a twenty-four-hour period shortens, and sleep becomes more concentrated in one long period at night. Babies three weeks of age sleep about sixteen hours per day and spend, on average, up to three and a half hours in a continuous episode of sleep; the longest episode of wakefulness is only about two hours. By the age of six months, babies spend only about half of a twenty-four-hour period sleeping, and their longest concentrated period of sleep is about five hours at night. In addition to relatively continuous night sleep, there are usually two shorter periods of sleep during the daytime hours. Sleep has been "consolidated," and the child is essentially sleeping through the night. When a child doesn't sleep through the night, she might make many or lengthy wake-up calls throughout the night or sleep mainly during the day. Children who continue having problems sleeping through the night may have sleep disturbances.

Many parents report that their baby sleeps "like an angel" from the day he came home from the hospital. Others describe sleep difficulties throughout their child's infancy. These reports indicate that differences related to sleep-wake patterns, or the tendency to suffer from sleep disorders, exist among babies owing to innate tendencies. According to some studies, although parents and other environmental factors have a huge influence on the development of children's sleep patterns, parents aren't necessarily "guilty" if their child develops a sleep disorder.

To understand the possible reasons for sleep disorders, we must become familiar with the processes and the variables that influence the natural development of sleep-wake patterns. Why, for example, does a baby's sleep concentrate during nighttime hours in one of the most rapid processes in the infant's first year of life? The answer to this question is related, among other things, to two more basic questions: Why are people daytime creatures and other mammals (such as the bat) nighttime creatures? What internal systems regulate each animal family's biological clock and determine whether it is a day animal or night animal?

The Biological Process

Two interconnected processes cause concentrated nighttime sleep: a biological process and an acquired social process. Man is a daytime creature. In terms of biology, we are "destined" to be awake and functioning by day and to sleep at night, as certain other animals have been "sentenced" to function as nighttime creatures or to reproduce during specific seasons of the year. Modern technology that has led to the development of artificial lighting, changes in cultural habits, leisure time at night, and the development of the need for nighttime activity has forced changes in sleep-wake patterns among many of us, but our biological inheritance remains the same.

Recent studies show that there is a well-developed system in our brain that signals us when to sleep and when to get up and go out to do our daily work in response to patterns of environmental light and darkness. The pineal gland has been identified as fulfilling a crucial role in producing information about day and night and relaying it to other centers in the brain. This gland has important functions for the reproductive system, controls the skin color of animals, and influences other neural systems. The pineal gland produces the hormone melatonin, which acts as a messenger that passes the sleep-wake signals on. Melatonin, also known as "the darkness hormone," was first identified in 1958, and many studies since have shown that it is secreted at night and inhibited by day, in both daytime and nighttime animals. Artificial lighting, however, apparently influences and confuses the patterns of melatonin secretion.

The study of animals has shown that melatonin is responsible for relaying information about cycles of light and darkness in the outside environment. It is also responsible for relaying information about the length of day and night, which is translated by animals into information about the seasons. When the time span during which melatonin is secreted is extended, for example, an animal "knows" that night is longer and that winter is approaching. This information is crucial to the animal's well-being, ensuring that animals mate according to seasonal patterns of fertility and that reproduction is indeed connected to a particular season. Farmers take advantage of this knowledge and use strong lighting in the winter in order to "trick" the hens. By producing a summer-like situation they increase their egg crop.

Many processes can be studied using artificially produced melatonin. Just as animals can be "tricked" into secreting a lower level of melatonin by controlled exposure to light, they can be "tricked" by the controlled injection of melatonin into their bloodstream. Farmers have learned to use this technique to control reproduction among animals. Melatonin in humans is also connected to many bodily and emotional processes. Very high levels of melatonin secretion, for instance, can inhibit women's ovulation. Other studies have shown that melatonin has a positive influence on some of the immune system's responses. Some theories suggest that melatonin can affect moods because of its link to the production of serotonin, a hormone that has an important role in depression.

Studies have shown that melatonin secretion will quickly be inhibited when a person is exposed during hours of darkness (when melatonin levels are high) to strong artificial light. In addition, administration of melatonin at different times of the day heightens a person's sleepiness.

Research and clinical studies have shown that blind people, both children and adults, tend to have difficulty falling asleep and awakening at nighttime — their biological clocks are out of sync. Apparently, their blindness prevents their brains from receiving necessary information about the external light-dark cycle. When patterns of melatonin secretion are examined in the blind, a strong link is indeed found between their sleep disturbances and faulty patterns of melatonin secretion. Significant success in treating the stubborn sleep disorders of blind children has been achieved by supplying them with controlled dosages of melatonin.

Melatonin in Infancy and Throughout Development

The recent increased interest in melatonin has led to a series of studies that have attempted to examine the patterns of its secretion throughout the life span. In these studies, the results show consistently that in the first months of a baby's life, levels of melatonin secretion are close to zero, and no kind of daily cycle can be demonstrated. In other words, nighttime secretion is no higher than daytime secretion. As the child approaches the age of six months, a gradual and significant increase in melatonin secretion begins to take place. Together with this increase, clear daily patterns are seen, highlighted by a peak of nighttime secretion and a relative inhibition of melatonin secretion during the day. Melatonin levels reach their peak at age four to six years, and then a gradual decrease in melatonin secretion begins and continues throughout life, so that melatonin levels are again very low among the elderly.

Sleep among the elderly is a particularly problematic and painful subject. In certain respects, the aged person completes the developmental cycle and returns to sleeping like a baby: sleep occurs in episodes throughout the day and night. Like the baby, the aged person has trouble maintaining continuous sleep throughout the night and naps frequently throughout the day. Dr. Iris Haimov, Professor Peretz Lavie, and associates at the Technion and Tel Aviv University investigated whether there is a relation between a drop in melatonin levels among the elderly and the sleep disturbances common to them. They discovered that those elderly who have especially low levels of melatonin are indeed those who suffer from significant sleep disorders. Elderly people who slept relatively well, on the other hand, had pineal glands that maintained high levels of melatonin production at night. These scientists also showed that administration of artificial melatonin can improve problematic sleep patterns of elderly people.

The discovery of these links between melatonin secretion and sleep consolidation has led my colleagues and me to wonder if these links also exist in early development. Is the formation of mature sleep patterns among babies in their first year of life linked to the pineal gland and the maturation of melatonin secretion patterns? We assumed that the baby's exposure to the environment's natural light and darkness, in conjunction with the formation of the neural system responsible for regulating the biological clock, significantly influences the baby's tendency to sleep at night and stay awake during the day. The initial results of a study that examined this question demonstrated that there is a strong connection between melatonin secretion patterns and the sleep patterns of a baby in the first year of life (see sidebar). We have concluded that the newborn's brain has a biological preparedness to mature and to prefer sleep at night and wakefulness during the day. The systems that influence this maturation process have become clearer in the past few years. This understanding will probably also aid in deciphering the reasons for some common childhood sleep disorders, especially those related to difficulty sleeping continuously throughout the night.

The Acquired Social Process

Parallel to biological forces, an entire system of environmental cues and "pressures" work on the baby. The average parent signals to the child in many ways that night is for sleeping and day is for wakeful activities. A parent usually responds quickly to a hungry baby during day-

Sleep and Melatonin Among Babies

In a study my colleagues and I recently conducted at Tel Aviv University, we examined the links between sleeping patterns and melatonin secretion among babies six to eight months of age. We asked parents to attach a "sleep watch" to their babies' ankles for a continuous week. At the same time, we asked them to keep the babies' disposable diapers in a cooler after use. We took urine samples from the used disposable diapers to determine the level of melatonin in the urine at different times of the day and night. The results of the study showed that babies who have more mature melatonin secretion patterns also have more mature sleep-wake patterns. As a baby's melatonin level increases toward evening, he tends to go to sleep earlier. We also found that babies whose patterns of melatonin secretion differed from the mature pattern suffered from more fragmented and interrupted sleep throughout the night. We concluded that development of the mature sleep-wake pattern is highly related to the maturation of melatonin secretion patterns. This link may explain why the development of sleep-wake patterns is delayed in some babies who suffer from sleep problems. It may also suggest that there is an underlying biological cause to some of the sleep problems seen during infancy.

time hours and happily supplies her with interesting stimuli. But parents are usually less patient at night. They maintain darkness and quiet in the baby's room and try to end any dialogue with the baby as quickly and efficiently as possible. These messages work as a system for reinforcing wakefulness during the day for the baby and discouraging behavior that promotes wakefulness at night. In many children with sleep disorders, we find that these signals are not detected by the child or are unclearly or inconsistently sent by the parents. It has been shown that when parents are trained, before or after the baby is born, to convey clear signals and expectations about sleep to their baby they can facilitate the development of good sleep habits and prevent or solve the common sleep problems of early childhood.

Because many factors influence infant sleep and many of these same factors are influenced by infant sleep, it is often difficult to disentangle the processes to understand which is the driving force and which the derivative. For instance, a number of studies have found a link between maternal depression and infant sleep problems. It is tempting to jump to the conclusion that a depressed mother with a compromised ability to respond to and care for the baby would cause her baby to be at a greater risk for developing a sleep problem. However, studies and clinical cases suggest that often a sleep-disturbed baby can lead his mother to the verge of exhaustion, despair, and a sense of helplessness that form the clinical picture of depression. Similar considerations should be applied to many of the factors described here, where the cause-and-effect relations are not simple or straightforward but more often involve a complex interaction and reciprocal effects.

4

"Why did my child laugh in his dream?"

The Significance and Roles of Dream-Sleep

We have learned how to identify the stage of dreaming in a
baby. If he is restless, with irregular breathing, if the tips of
his fingers move in short, quick
or jerky movements, if his eyes
quickly scurry from side to side and twitches or
smiles appear on his face — then he is in the midst
of dream sleep. Does this mean that the child is really dreaming? A baby cannot report on her dreams
because of her limited verbal ability. Even young
children who do have a reasonable command of language have difficulty relating to the dream experience and distinguishing between it and reality. How,
then, can we know that a baby dreams? We cannot
know for certain, but we infer it based on a number
of facts from research on children, adults, and animals.

With the discovery that babies dream, and the
awareness that a similar phenomenon occurs among
adults, researchers examined these phenomena in
sleep laboratories. As we have seen, it has been
found that if an adult is awakened during REM sleep,
the chance that he will report that he was dreaming
is very high (about 70 percent). On the other hand,

if the same person is awakened during a different stage of sleep, the chance of his reporting that he dreamed is low (20–30 percent). That is why the stage of sleep characterized by the special physiological activity of rapid eye movements, increased brain activity, and very low muscle tone was termed dream-sleep. Dream-sleep is also called paradoxical sleep, because the brain works in high gear while the body is motionless, like a driver revving up a car engine while the gear is in neutral. Still, it is important to remember that dreaming can occur in quiet sleep as well as in dream-sleep.

In studies on cats, operations were performed in the area of the brain responsible for inhibiting movement of the limbs and the body during dream-sleep. The result was that each time a cat entered dream-sleep, it began to perform typical movements resembling sexual activity or aggressive or defensive behaviors. These studies led to the hypothesis that dream-sleep serves as practice for significant activity patterns, while the movement suppression protects the dreamer from dangers inherent in unrestricted motion linked to the dream. These studies also indirectly supported Freud's theory concerning the role of dreams. According to Freud, dreams are meant to allow a covert expression of such basic drives as sexuality and aggressiveness. Freud believed that the direct waking expression of these drives stirs up anxiety and panic and therefore is repressed. In sleep, too, according to Freud, the direct expression of these drives stirs up feelings that could lead to awakening. The covert expression of these urges in the form of a dream protects the continuity of sleep. Freud believed that nightmares and dreams that wake the sleeper are examples of the failure of the function of the dream to protect sleep.

Although the study of dreams in babies and young children is limited by the subject's minimal ability to report, the role of dream-sleep can be studied indirectly by quantitatively examining the duration of "active sleep" over the course of development. Babies spend a lot of time in dream-sleep. During their first weeks of life, a baby spends about half of his sleeping time in dream-sleep — an average of approximately eight hours daily. With age, a gradual decrease in dream-sleep occurs. An older child spends only about two hours out of twenty-four in dream-sleep. Older children and adults spend a significant amount of time in different stages of sleep before entering the first episode of dream-sleep, while babies usually enter dream sleep as soon as they fall asleep.

Babies' greater need for dream-sleep is related to the fact that humans are born with an immature central nervous system. The human baby is born with a brain that weighs about one fourth as much as an adult brain. As a result, the human baby is critically dependent on the environment — in particular, the parents — in order to survive. Many animal newborns, on the other hand, are born almost fully developed physically and neurologically and can function just like adults almost immediately after their birth. A crucial factor in the brain's maturation is intensive neural activity. While in dream-sleep, the brain works intensely, sometimes even more so than during wakefulness. This is probably how the electrical-neural stimulation necessary for development is supplied.

From an evolutionary point of view, a close inverse relation exists between the amount of dream-sleep of an animal and the degree of its childhood brain maturation. Rats and cats, for example, spend 80–90 percent of their sleep in dream sleep at the beginning of life but only 20–30 percent with brain maturation. Animals that are born with a mature brain, on the other hand, such as guinea pigs and sheep, spend relatively little time in dream-sleep from the first days of their lives, and the percentage does not change significantly with age.

Because mental activity is accelerated in dream-sleep, and because we remember part of the contents of dreams, some scientists have suggested the possibility that dreams play a part in information integration processes that occur during wakefulness. The perceptual system responsible for reception, integration, and recollection of information is a complex one that takes in a tremendous amount of information from the environment and from the body and its sensations. Part of the processing is done during wakefulness, when the system is bombarded with external stimuli, but a different and crucial part must be performed when the system is disconnected from external stimuli. During sleep, the brain is relatively disconnected from the environment. And indeed, in research on children and adults, much evidence has suggested that dream-sleep functions in processing the information perceived during wakefulness and in the storage in the long-term memory. The phenomenon can be compared to a librarian who during library hours has to assist patrons in finding, borrowing, and returning books; only after the library closes does the librarian have an opportunity to catalog, sort, and reshelve the books. As a child grows and his central nervous system matures, it is able to cope with information reception and integration during wakefulness and demands less integration time during sleep (dream-sleep). There is evidence that the amount of dream-sleep is directly influenced by the amount of learning done before sleep. It has also been found that when dream-sleep is selectively prevented by waking the dreamer each time that he enters the stage of dream-sleep, his learning is damaged and he "forgets" the new material learned.

Brain maturation is responsible for the inhibition of

movements during sleep in general and during dream-sleep in particular. This gradual maturation helps explain why babies in their first months of life are much more active than older babies. This also explains why body movements at the tips of the limbs and facial muscular activity (twitching or smiling) are evident during dream-sleep. And indeed, a baby's charming smile appears during dream-sleep as a nonsocial pattern long before it appears during wakefulness in a social context, as a response to those around him. It seems that the same muscular activity appears in dream-sleep in an automatic manner as a by-product of neural activity, not because the baby was necessarily dreaming about something funny. This scientific explanation, however, should not diminish the joy experienced by many parents who believe their baby is having a pleasant or entertaining experience while asleep.

In order to peek into the content of early childhood dreams, we can look at studies done on children two to three years old who begin to tell about their dreams. The dreams of these children are characterized by brevity, relative lack of expressed emotions, and simplicity. Many dreams deal with animals, and a small percentage deal directly with parents or other key figures. Many dreams focus on some need of the child (such as hunger or thirst) or a different wish. Many children's (and adults') dreams feature recently encountered subjects or experiences. An example is the first dream that one of my daughters told me about when she was two and a half years old. She dreamed that she had gotten lost in a forest and couldn't find her way to Mommy or Daddy. This dream occurred the night after she had lost eye contact with her parents in a big store and had panicked for a few minutes. In this case, the event that led to the dream can be easily identified. My daughter's anxiety from the previous day's

The Meaning of Dreams According to Psychoanalysis

In 1900 Freud published *The Interpretation of Dreams*. This book, considered a significant breakthrough in understanding dreams and the processes that occur during them, was one of the foundations of psychoanalysis. Freud asserted that dreams are a sort of window for our wishes and drives that do not find expression or release in wakeful life. In addition, Freud described the thought processes in dreams, which work not according to the rules of logic and the accepted perceptions among adults but according to symbolic relations motivated primarily by drives and wishes ("primary thought"). The rules of thought that are at work during sleep characterize, among other things, the life of our imagination, the thoughts of young children, artists in the process of creating, or part of the disturbed thought processes of emotionally disturbed people. Freud believed that most drives and wishes that are expressed in dreams are related to aggression or sexuality and are not given direct expression due to social and personal limitations that "censor" them during the wakeful day. The central censoring control relaxes during sleep and allows expression of these urges, sometimes in a direct manner but usually indirectly, via symbols. In dreams these drives are largely obscured because of taboos. Since Freud, the understanding of the meaning of dreams has been elaborated by many theories and much scientific research.

Still, there is wide agreement that dreams are stories written by the dreamer when control and logic play a smaller role than in wakefulness. Dreams can thus teach us about the emotional world of the dreamer. Psychologists who use dream interpretation as a tool in the process of psychotherapy share this perception.

event had continued to bother her. It was not expressed in other behaviors during the following day, but it was expressed in her dream. In many cases, subjects or experiences can bother the child without his or our conscious knowledge, and dreams can be a window to the hidden inner emotional life of the child.

"A child who doesn't sleep doesn't grow"

Sleep and Physical Growth

The physical growth of the baby (weight, height, and head circumference) is one of the primary concerns of parents, and of professionals who try to detect babies and young children who are at high developmental or medical risk. One standard test done as a follow-up at well-mother and -baby clinics is weighing and measuring the height of the child and comparing the measurements to the expected growth curve. The growth curve takes the basic data of length and weight development into account, giving the maximum variance among babies according to these measures. The follow-up of the growth curve of the child allows identification of unexpected delay in growth. When a delay is detected, of course, the source of the problem must be identified. On the other hand, tracking the child's growth can show that he is developing as expected, thereby reassuring parents who may be concerned that their child isn't eating enough. It may also hearten mothers who fear they don't have enough milk to nurse their babies and are thereby failing to meet the child's most basic need.

According to an old wives' tale, "If you don't

sleep enough, you won't grow" — an intuitive association between sleep and physical growth. Just as with some other folk sayings, it took science years of research to discover that this adage contains a grain of truth. In the 1960s Japanese scientists reported that the growth hormone of young children is secreted mainly during sleep, with peak secretion occurring early in the night, during condensed stages of deep sleep. In other words, a strong relation indeed exists between the processes of sleep and physical growth. On the other hand, no conclusive proof exists that the amount or quality of sleep directly affects growth. Studies and clinical evidence suggest rather that only the most difficult sleep disorders can trigger a growth disturbance. Severe sleep disorders — for example, those that stem from respiratory disorders during sleep — can lead to growth disturbances. An acceleration of physical growth has been reported among some children after successful treatment for respiratory disorders brought about a substantial improvement in the quality of sleep. Even in these cases, it is unclear whether the sleep disorder was the main reason for the growth disturbance or whether a third variable caused both the sleep disorder and the growth disturbance — for instance, emotional neglect, which is known to be a potential cause of growth disturbances and sleep disorders (see sidebar).

The links between sleep and body size have also been investigated in infants and young children who suffer from sleep apnea because of enlarged tonsils or adenoids. Sleep apnea is a severe breathing problem during sleep that causes significant sleep disruptions. When children with sleep apnea were treated by surgically removing their enlarged tonsils and adenoids, their sleep improved. In addition, their height and weight increased significantly. At least two possible explanations can account for this increase in body size. First, when children sleep bet-

Psychological Aspects of Physical Growth

Physical growth is related to physiological mechanisms, nutrition, and processes of maturation. But it is also important to consider the influence of psychological and environmental variables on growth. Much evidence suggests that the emotional environment in which a child grows up influences the rate of her growth. One phenomenon in which the emotional environment negatively influences a child's growth is called failure to thrive.

Some studies have shown that failure to thrive may result from the mother's difficulty in feeding the baby, from neglect or parental abuse, or from the mother's emotional problems in her relationship with her baby. Other researchers hold that growth disturbances result from unidentified neurological disorders. We must remember that problems in the relationship between mother and child may be the result of, not the reason for, the stress inherent in coping with a child's growth disturbance of unknown origin.

In a study my colleagues and I conducted on preschool and elementary school children in Bradley Hospital, a psychiatric pediatric facility in Providence, Rhode Island, we found that children who were sexually abused were physically smaller than other children their age. Although we did not find a direct correlation between sleep problems among the children and their physical growth, the sleep disorders prevalent among children who experienced sexual trauma in childhood may explain, in certain cases, the delay in growth.

ter they expend less energy; second, the secretion from their growth hormone could have been normalized, thus leading to a general growth acceleration.

Studies of children who do not suffer from severe sleep disorders do not usually point to a significant relation between duration of sleep and physical growth. This said, we must remember that duration of sleep becomes shorter over the course of our lifetime, parallel to a decrease in the rate of physical growth. In adolescence, an accelerated stage of bodily development, a significant change in sleep patterns has been found in the form of an increased need to sleep and increased daytime sleepiness. It is possible that the accelerated growth requires increased expenditure of body energy, and therefore the body requires more sleep in order to recuperate.

Although we emphasize the effects of sleep disruptions on physical growth, it is important to remember that body size can have significant effects on sleep. Obese children and adults are at a greater risk of breathing-related sleep problems. These problems usually result from obstructions to the airways that allow breathing during sleep. Similar to other factors associated with sleep, the relations between sleep and body size are complex and reciprocal. It is important to reassure parents that the common sleep problems of bedtime struggles and night-wakings do not lead to a growth failure. Nevertheless, there are other good reasons why these should be treated.

6

"He's hyperactive, and at night he has trouble falling asleep"

Sleep, Personality, and Behavior of the Baby

A leading researcher on temperament in infants and young children once said in despair, "When I raised my first child, I believed behavioral theories claiming that what I do as a parent molds my child's character. With my second child, I was already a geneticist and believed that a child is born with characteristics that are passed on through heredity and that environmental influence is minimal. I barely knew my third child at all . . ." This analysis was, of course, exaggerated, but it demonstrates the ongoing quest of parents and scientists to answer the question, What determines the personality and personal characteristics of the child? The question of heredity ("She got her shyness from her dad's family") versus environment ("If his mother were more strict with him, he would be calmer") underlies parents' attempts to understand the range of influence they have in molding their paragon creation — their child.

Up-to-date research points to a complex picture vis-à-vis the influence of heredity and environment on the child. Much evidence suggests that the baby is born with genetic baggage that not only determines how he looks, the color of his eyes, and his chances of suffering from various diseases but also significantly influences the character traits that he will develop. Physical activity level, shyness or sociability, openness to new situations, and anxiety are among the traits that are related to the genetic predisposition with which babies enter the world.

Many parents discover that their child has traits that are undesirable to them — especially if they remind them of qualities they dislike about their parents, their spouses, or themselves. Parents frequently try to fight these traits, and they often discover that it is a losing battle. It seems that the most important variable that influences the quality of relationship between parents and children is the "goodness of fit" between the child's traits and the parents' expectations. A very active child, for example, may be adored by a father who appreciates and identifies with this trait but merely tolerated by a father who expects a calmer child. On the other hand, a quiet, calm child may be considered depressive or lifeless by the first father, while the second father sees her as perfect. Incompatibility between parental expectations and the child's traits may lead to frustration and stress in the relationship, particularly if the parents try to "correct" the child to conform to their expectations.

Compatibility between the child's sleep patterns and the parents' expectations is another key element of the relationship. A child who goes to sleep early and wakes up early in the morning, refreshed and ready for a new day, may not be compatible with the parent whose inclination is to "sleep in." Some claim, in fact, that infants don't suffer from sleep problems, that only their parents do. In practice, though, the identification of a sleep problem is based on both the actual sleep patterns of the child and the tolerance or intolerance of the parents to those patterns.

The Relation Between Temperament and Sleep

Every parent is familiar with the situation in which her child demonstrates by his behavior that he "is up past his bedtime." When we asked parents to describe this situation, some said that the child calms down, seems sleepy, falls asleep on his own, or asks directly or indirectly to go to bed. Other parents said that their child in this situation "climbs the walls," "is a crybaby," "is nervous and unhappy with everything," "doesn't respond to what he's told," or "does annoying things to spite us."

Clearly, young children react to tiredness in significantly different ways. A state of fatigue is not necessarily expressed by decreased activity and obvious sleepiness. Sometimes the symptoms can be just the opposite. Some of the typical "negative" behaviors of the tired child are compatible with general patterns that characterize behavior disorders.

Much evidence points to a strong correlation between sleep and the development of the child's personality traits. Studies have shown that a baby who suffers from sleep disorders (difficulty falling asleep, for example, or many awakenings during the night) tends to be "more difficult" in other behavioral domains. In a study my colleagues and I conducted in the Sleep Laboratory at the Technion, we compared a group of nine- to twenty-four-month-old babies whose parents had come for consultation about their children's sleep problems with a control group of babies without sleep disorders. We found significant differences in traits that the mothers attributed to their babies. The mothers completed a temperament questionnaire, which is a sort of "personality" test for young children. The mothers rated their degree of agreement with such sentences as "The child agrees to be dressed and undressed without protesting," "The child responds strongly (screams, yells) when frustrated," and "The child sits quietly when waiting to eat." In general, the mothers of babies with sleep problems described them as more demanding, complaining, annoying, negatively sensitive to different stimuli, and difficult to adapt to different situations, as compared with babies without sleep problems.

One of the traits measured in the temperament questionnaire is the degree of sensitivity or responsivity of the baby to different sensory stimuli (noise, temperature, taste, smell). Some babies are very sensitive to any kind of sensory stimulus, and others are sensitive only to a specific type of sensation — for example, those who recoil from skin contact. A wide range of babies do not respond in an outstanding way to sensory stimuli. One of the hypotheses that the researcher William Carey examined in 1974 was that babies who suffer from hypersensitivity to sensory stimuli would tend to develop sleep difficulties. Carey's findings supported the hypothesis, and he claimed that the heightened sensitivity to sensory stimuli is hereditary. In order to fall asleep, the baby has to disassociate himself from the external environment and stop responding to people, noise, light, and temperature, and to disassociate from internal signals as well, such as pain, discomfort, and hunger.

This ability to disassociate is most critical for maintaining uninterrupted sleep and for preventing awakenings in response to various stimuli. A baby who is sensitive from birth to any internal or external stimulus will have trouble disassociating from environmental stimuli, which will interfere with his ability to relax and fall asleep easily and will cause him to awaken easily and frequently over the course of the night. In our study, we too found a strong correlation between babies' sensory sensitivities and the sleep difficulties that characterized them.

This correlation between sleep and behavior continues throughout later childhood. Studies that examined school-aged children found a correlation between sleep disorders and problems with behavior and more general adaptation. Actually, sleep disorders serve as a sensitive barometer of general adaptation problems among children and adults. Sleep disorders are a prominent sign of stress and anxiety, depression, and adaptation problems. Sleep problems are so prevalent in some behavior or emotional disorders that they have been included in diagnostic criteria. One factor that strengthens a diagnosis of anxiety disorders in a child, for example, is the presence of a sleep disorder.

The close correlation between sleep disorders and behavior problems in children can be explained in a number of ways. Perhaps a child born with a tendency toward problematic behavior develops sleep problems as well, as a result. At the same time, it is reasonable to infer that significant sleep problems will lead to insufficient sleep or sleep deprivation, which may cause the child to be nervous, impatient, and harder to manage. In addition, a third cause, such as incompatible parenting patterns, may provoke or aggravate both behavior problems and sleep difficulties.

In treatment centers, we frequently come across babies or young children who are described by their parents as hyperactive. The parents use this term casually, but professionals use it to diagnose a condition — the professional term is attention deficit hyperactivity disorder — that occurs only in older children. These babies are described as especially active and restless and are said to demand attention and seek stimuli constantly. Often parents associate their child's sleep difficulties with his wakeful restlessness. Occasionally a parent says something like, "This boy has a turbo engine and he cannot shut it down at bedtime," or "He is like the Energizer bunny; he keeps going and going and going."

Although hyperactivity is diagnosed at a later age, there is evidence that most hyperactive children were overactive, restless babies, with difficult temperaments. Again, we face a chicken-or-egg question: are these babies unable to sleep like "normal" babies because they are unusually active, or does their sleep problem underlie their "hyperactivity"? In many cases sleep disruption appears to lead to "hyperactive" behavior patterns, even though no research has directly substantiated this clinical impression. More and more evidence demonstrates that lack of sleep may bring on behavior that resembles that of a hyperactive child. From an intuitive perspective we can all recall methods we use to keep ourselves awake when we are tired. These methods include increasing our activity, fidgeting, fiddling with our hands or our facial muscles, and similar strategies. This pattern contradicts the expectation that the tired child will relax and slow down. The clinical literature has documented certain cases in which significant sleep problems have been found to lead to "hyperactive" behavior patterns and later to an erroneous diagnosis and treatment. It is of utmost importance to examine the possibility that the sleep disorder is the source and not the outcome of the "hyperactivity." In the event that a sleep disorder exists, it should be treated before treating the disorders that result from it. In some cases treating the sleep disorder may spare the child from receiving unnecessary medication like Ritalin, which is the most prescribed chemical response to children's behavioral problems.

An erroneous interpretation of child's behavior can also result when she responds to a sleep disorder with heightened tiredness, indifference, and lack of interest in the environment. This pattern may be interpreted as depression, and the sleep difficulties can be seen as the result of that condition. As the professional literature reveals, such an erroneous diagnosis can result in a failure to detect and treat a primary sleep disorder, as well as mistaken treatment for depression. Case studies have shown that when the problem is diagnosed correctly as a primary sleep disorder and treated accordingly, there is a parallel improvement in sleep and disappearance of the "depressive" symptoms.

Intellectual Development

Assessing intelligence in infancy is a very complex task. Tests used on infants to assess early mental abilities that could be considered components of intelligence have generally failed to predict intelligence or cognitive abilities and achievements in later ages. The research on the relation between sleep and intellectual development has been hampered by our limited capacity to assess intelligence in infants. Efforts to study this issue have failed to provide a clear picture of the situation, and we need to call upon additional studies on older children and adults to help us consider the issue more systematically.

Scientists from the University of Connecticut in Evelyn Thoman's group, which has contributed significantly to the field of the study of infant sleep, examined this question. They followed sleep of newborns over the course of their first two days of life and examined their development at the age of six months. Special recording devices documented the babies' sleep in hospital bassinets after birth. The scientists then tested the mental, motor, and perceptual abilities of the babies at the age of six months, using the Bayley Test. They found a correlation between sleep measures of the newborns on their first day of life and their development six months later.

Some scientists found a correlation between sleep disorders in infancy, especially those that are caused by respiratory problems, and possible shortfalls in intellectual development and academic achievements at a later age. Other studies, however, found no comprehensible correlation between sleep and later mental function.

Studies on older children and adults have shown that sleep disorders or insufficient sleep primarily interfere with cognitive abilities associated with attention and concentration. That is to say that the ability to focus on certain stimuli for extended time deteriorates. People who don't get enough sleep react more slowly and make more mistakes on tasks that demand attention and continuous concentration. Although the question of sleep and attention has not been directly studied in infants, some support for their correlation comes from indirect approaches. For example, mothers described their babies (aged nine to twenty-four months) who suffered from sleep problems as having trouble concentrating on play or a particular activity for an extended length of time, and as easily distracted by other stimuli.

In another recent study, my colleagues and I examined the relation between sleep patterns and learning skills, concentration, and attention among school-aged children. The sleep patterns of the children were examined objectively by using sleep watches, and their learning functions were examined by computerized tests. Similar to the results in studies of adults, we found that children whose quality of sleep deteriorated (as manifested by many or lengthy awakenings from sleep during the night) also had decreased attention abilities. These findings support the assumption that these critical functions for learning and academic achievement are adversely affected by sleep disorders among children. Furthermore, recent studies have shown that if "normal" children are requested to shorten their sleep for experimental purposes, they suffer negative consequences, and their learning and attention abilities are significantly compromised.

On the basis of what we have learned about older children and adults and from the limited information on infants, it is fair to conclude that the intellectual abilities of infants are challenged by disrupted or insufficient sleep. Such important questions as what the long-term consequences of these conditions are still wait for a systematic investigation.

7

"She refuses to go to sleep ever since she awoke from a scary nightmare"

Infant Sleep in Stressful Situations

Sleep is the most sensitive barometer of emotional stress, tension, and anxiety. Most of us can retrieve the memory of a past significant event that disrupted our sleep. We may have had trouble falling asleep the night before an important examination or some other exciting event. There have been nights before an important meeting when we've awakened several times to make sure the alarm clock didn't "forget" to wake us up. After these events passed, sleep resumed normal patterns as if nothing had happened. Why is sleep so vulnerable to stressful situations, and how do babies respond to them?

Parents who consult me about their baby's sleep usually demonstrate a great deal of sensitivity about physical issues and their possible influence on her sleep. Parents may view the child's sleep problems as related to illness, nutrition, teething, or clothing, for example. Some parents seem unaware of the possibility that the baby's sleep may be disturbed due to emotional distress or anxiety. But a detailed inquiry often reveals that the child's sleep problems began at the same time that she exhibited signs of separation anxiety, underwent a change in lifestyle (a new caretaker or day-care center, for example), or observed a situation in which her parents were under stress. Babies absorb and react to these conditions without even understanding their significance.

A typical example of such reaction is the case of Susan, who sought treatment with her three-year-old daughter Lisa. Susan came to see me because Lisa had begun to awaken at night over the past two months, demanding her mother's presence at her bedside to help her return to sleep. Some nights Lisa would join her mother in her parents' bed in the middle of the night, remaining there until morning. At our first meeting, Susan was unable to pinpoint a reason why this problem had cropped up. Lisa had been a good sleeper previously. But when asked about stressful situations in the family, Susan told me that her mother had died three months before and that she was going through a difficult grieving process because she had shared a special relationship with her mother. When the evaluation of Lisa's sleep revealed no other likely causes of her sleep problem, my inquiry focused on Susan's relationship with her mother.

At this point Susan observed that during the first phase of her grieving, she was in a state of deep sadness, frequently crying in Lisa's presence. Lisa even learned to say "Mommy is sad" in response to her mother's dark moods and crying. I suspected that Lisa had absorbed her mother's distress and responded by wanting to "care for" her, to be close to her and soothe her. This pattern was especially expressed as a desire to be close to her mother at night. Susan responded positively, due to her own need for closeness and as a step toward getting on with her life after her mother's death. This pattern between mother and daughter, created during Susan's period of emotional distress, seemed to have become a habit that continued even after she had recovered from her grief. Based on this hypothesis, Susan felt that she could clarify to Lisa that it was time to return to her regular sleep pattern in her own room. Susan considered using "prizes" to reinforce success in the process. But to her surprise, just one night after she explained the plan to Lisa, the problem disappeared as if it had never existed. My impression was that Lisa immediately understood that she could stop her "night watch" over her mother and reacted by changing the habit right away, with no fights or special resistance.

This example illustrates the acute sensitivity of babies and young children to their parents' emotional circumstances, and how those circumstances can cause stress that influences the children's functioning. Many parents believe that their child is too young to comprehend their emotional situation, and that if they refrain from talking about it in her presence, she will not absorb and react to it. In fact, although the child cannot understand the complex conditions the parents face, she is most skilled in absorbing and reacting to sensitive situations of the people most significant to her. A parent's stressful situation may thus quickly trigger the child's stressful reaction. And the stressful reaction is often expressed as a sleep problem.

The topic of stress is one of the most complex and most researched fields of psychology. Stressful situations and reactions to them are considered the major causes of adaptation problems and psychopathology in childhood and adulthood. A stressful situation is defined as a significant event that requires the expenditure of emotional and physical resources for the person to adapt and continue functioning at a normal level. Some external events — for example, war and natural disasters — are commonly perceived as stress producing for all who experience them. Other situations are stressful only for some people.

The primary causes of stress among young babies are related to the physiological regulation of their needs. Fatigue, pain, and such sources of physical discomfort as hunger, thirst, heat, and cold create stress. John Bowlby and other researchers have also emphasized the baby's basic need for emotional attachment to her mother as a protecting and warm figure. Their studies demonstrated the importance of satisfaction of these psychological needs. In extreme situations, when babies were separated from their mothers and had no substitute to connect to, they deteriorated into such severe depressive states that they lost their appetites and signs of vitality; some of these babies even died.

Little research has been done on stressful events for babies and children, largely because of the ethical problems inherent in creating controlled stress or distress among babies. It is difficult to justify a study that puts a child into a stressful situation when we assume that the stress will have negative ramifications for the child. In order to examine the influence of daily stressful events on a baby's sleep, scientists use mildly stressful situations or stresses that arise naturally in a child's life. Spending the night in a sleep laboratory for a medical examination, for example, is a stressful event that demands a certain adaptation, even among adults. Individuals routinely sleep worse during the first night in the laboratory than on subsequent nights, because they must adapt to the new arrangement. Scientists in the United States tested the differences in babies' sleeping patterns between the first period in a laboratory sleep examination, when they were not yet used to the equipment and their new environment, and an additional period, after they had had time to adjust to the new arrangement. The researchers found that they could not initially determine among young babies aged two weeks and eight weeks a daily distribution of sleep that would point to a preference for nighttime sleep over daytime sleep, as we would expect to find among very young babies. Only after the babies had gone through an adjustment period could their preference for continuous nighttime sleep be identified in their sleep patterns. The scientists concluded that the stressful situation and the laboratory circumstances disrupted the sleep patterns the babies had attained in a natural setting. Normal sleep preferences were expressed only a month after their adaptation to laboratory conditions.

One unique study that dealt with babies' and young children's sleep in stressful situations was conducted by Professor Peretz Lavie and colleagues in the sleep laboratory of the Technion during the Persian Gulf war. Thirty-eight of thirty-nine missiles that Iraq launched at civilian population centers in Israel were fired at night. Although damage to the population was minimal, many homes were badly damaged. There was also considerable concern that the missiles might bear deadly chemicals and that civilians unharmed by the explosions might later suffer death or illness. Warnings of attacks were broadcast only one or two minutes before the missiles landed. During these attacks, civilians were requested to remain in a specially designed sealed room, to wear gas masks, and to put their babies into a special protective tent. Because almost all the missiles were launched at night, a variety of fears arose regarding possible attack while asleep. Reports of sleep difficulties among the adult population intensified these fears.

The study was intended to examine the influence of stresses arising from the gulf war children's sleep and was conducted using two sleep-assessment methods. The first method, which focused on a population that had been studied before the war, was to distribute questionnaires to parents about their babies' sleep before the war and after its conclusion. The second method was to record the children's sleep, using sleep watches, over the course of a continuous week during the war. The questionnaire-based sleep measures did not show significant differences between the babies' sleep patterns before and after the war. The data from the sleep watches showed that the children woke up for a brief period as a reaction to the missiles' impact but resumed sleeping immediately after the event and showed no specific signs of distress or sleep disturbance.

These results are quite surprising. How is it possible that such a stressful, life-threatening event, which takes place during the night and disrupts family sleeping arrangements, doesn't leave a significant mark on children's sleep? One possible explanation is that for young children, unable to comprehend the full danger of the situation, a gathering in a sealed room can be perceived as a "family party," with the parents trying to soothe and pamper them. In other words, it may be that children did not experience these events as stressful or fearful whatsoever, because they perceived and interpreted the events differently than did adults.

In a similar study, which was conducted using sleep watches on an adult population in Israel, no significant influences of wartime events were found on objective sleep measures. Nonetheless, many complaints were reported by adults about fear of sleeping and difficulties related to sleep. In other words, sleep did not objectively change among adults; rather, the significant change was in their perception of sleep.

Obviously, even based on as representative a sample as can be, conclusions cannot confidently be applied to the population at large. A number of parents who turn to me for treatment of their children's sleep disorders are certain that the source of the problem is the child's experiences as a "sealed-room baby." Again, reliable conclusions cannot be drawn about the relation between stressful war-related experiences and the sleep disorder, even though these parents naturally tend to link the events.

Studies of older children and adults point to two response patterns to stressful situations. One is a pattern of alarm, restlessness, agitation, nervousness, and increased vocalization, which is associated with increased vigilance and sleep difficulties. This pattern is explained as an ongoing attempt to actively cope with and change the stressful situation, whether by directly altering it or by signaling distress to caretakers, to get them to change the situation. The second pattern observed in stressful situations, especially uncontrollable ones that are prolonged or chronic, is a passive-repressive pattern. This pattern is expressed in decreased activity, isolation of emotions, shutting oneself in, and escaping into extended and deep sleep. This pattern apparently serves as protection against a stressful situation that seems impossible to change. As far as can be discerned, these two characteristic response patterns have opposite ramifications for sleep. In the first pattern, sleep negates the ability to directly cope with stress and danger and therefore is significantly disturbed. In the second pattern, sleep is an escape from the causes of the stress and is therefore intensified.

8

"It's hard for me to abandon him alone in bed"

The Meaning of Sleep for Children and Parents

Going to sleep is the most significant daily separation of a baby from his parents. The parents, or significant others, have been in constant contact with the child throughout the day, responding to his every wish and attending to whatever was botheringhim. Suddenly the situation changes: the parents cut off contact and in many cases expect their child to spend the night alone in a separate room, with minimal communication. The separation, which is part of the putting-to-bed and going-to-sleep ritual, has many different meanings for parents and babies. In most cases it is a good separation that manifests the parents' confidence in themselves and acknowledgment of the baby's need to be able to calm himself down and sleep. The separation and the new meeting each morning confirm and strengthen the baby's and the parents' confidence in their separate existence even when there is no eye contact or physical touch or closeness. The consistency of this cyclical process makes it predictable and therefore safe. Disruptions of the process, however, frequently arise: the baby may develop separation anxiety (a natural developmental occurrence), or parents may have their own trouble with the process at times.

The newborn baby is an immature creature that is totally dependent on his mother (or another primary care giver) for his existence. This period of dependency continues until an independent existence begins to be achieved. The mother goes through emotional and physiological processes that prepare her to respond to the baby's needs. These processes begin during pregnancy, reach their peak at birth, and gradually decline as the child develops. The renowned pediatrician and psychoanalyst D. W. Winnicott, who described these processes, emphasized the huge emotional and cognitive stake that a mother invests in her baby in the first months of his life, giving up, to a great degree, her own needs and other aspects of her life.

The baby is born with many talents for finding and identifying the human figures that help her survive. She is able to signal needs, distress, and satisfaction to her mother. She can cry differently to signal hunger or pain, and she can smile to express satisfaction and comfort when all her needs are met. From the moment of birth, the baby displays clear preferences about things she sees, hears, smells, and feels. Although we used to believe that the newborn baby is passive, unable to see, helpless, and sensorily restricted, modern research has shown that these conclusions stemmed from the limitations of earlier research methods or our limited abilities to distinguish the sophisticated talents of the baby. As research methods have become more advanced, the newborn baby's abilities have become increasingly evident.

The attachment to a maternal figure who cares for the baby is an existential need that is crucial for the baby's normal development. During the first few months of life, a normally developing baby does not exhibit a unique response to a brief separation from her mother or at the appearance of unfamiliar people. However, when separation anxiety arrives, it can become a powerful source of problems in normal development. This anxiety, which normally appears at age eight to ten months, symbolizes the beginning of the baby's growing awareness of physical separateness from her mother. The accepted explanation is that in the first months of life it is hard for the baby to distinguish between her actions and thoughts and those of others in her environment, especially her mother. The same physical oneness that existed in the womb continues to exist for the baby for several months after birth. Only gradually, after countless activities and interactions with the environment, does the baby become aware that she is a separate being who is greatly dependent on another. The baby's feelings of separateness and dependence can be expressed during the day by such reactions as clinging or anger, and by dissociation after separation. The child's stress responses after separation put heavy emotional pressure on the parents and may make them fear and refrain from additional significant separations.

Separation anxiety is one of the main causes of sleep disorders in early childhood. The baby who is in close contact with his parents during his waking hours must go to sleep and quickly adapt to a situation of no physical contact with them. The rise in the frequency of sleeping disorders during the first year of life may be linked to the appearance of the separation anxiety that is a normal developmental occurrence at this age.

In the clinic, many parents report on the appearance of sleep problems based on some significant separation. A change such as the mother's return to work after maternity leave, a new caretaker, the transition to day care, or any change that signifies separation and a new adaptation is frequently expressed immediately in the form of a significant sleep disorder.

A baby's or young animal's typical response pattern to separation from its mother has unique features. This pattern is observed both in monkeys and in humans in both experimental studies and in follow-up studies of natural situations. A reaction pattern is characterized in the first stage by heightened irritability, increased physical activity, and increased crying, calling out, and other vocalizations. In the second stage a depressive reaction appears, manifested in a decrease in activity and, in cases of longer separations, a loss of appetite, apathy, and lack of responsiveness to the environment.

For obvious ethical reasons, a controlled study of the reactions of human babies to extended separation from their parents cannot be carried out. Typical studies of this phenomenon examine the baby's immediate reactions to a brief separation from the mother. For example, psychologists observe the degree to which the child is distressed in a "strange situation" — as when the mother leaves him with an unfamiliar adult and exits the room for a few minutes — and how he responds to her return after the separation. Studies that have examined a longer separation from the mother have taken advantage of real-life situations, or have observed monkeys, which are the closest animals to humans on the evolutionary scale. The results of studies with young monkeys showed many physiologic responses to lengthy separations from their mothers or from other monkeys their own age with whom they were raised. These responses are characteristic of several types of monkeys. The physiologic responses included changes and disorders in heartbeat and body temperature, damage to the immune system, and an increase in secretion of stress hormones. Sleep disturbances were also found, manifest by numerous night wakings, changes in dream-sleep, and other changes in brain waves during sleep.

A relation between separation from the mother and sleep disturbances has also been seen among babies and young children. In a series of studies that were done on the reactions of babies and young children to a temporary separation from their mothers, Prof. Tiffany Field and colleagues showed that responses to stress among babies are expressed in their sleep patterns. For example, the responses of sixteen children ranging in age from twenty-two months to five years were examined when their mothers were in the hospital giving birth to another child. The children were examined before, during, and after their mothers' hospitalization. The results of the study showed that during the mothers' hospitalization, the children fell asleep more quickly and slept longer in general and particularly in deep sleep. The children also woke up more often, however, and cried more during the night. The scientists explained their findings by saying that deep and lengthier sleep is part of a regressive pattern that helps conserve energy. This is a typical response pattern of animals and humans to prolonged stress that cannot be controlled or stopped. The prolific night wakings and crying were explained as additional distress signals of children during their mothers' hospitalization. The sleep-behavior changes can be explained as well by the fact that the fathers of the children cared for them in the mothers' absence, presumably adopting a different caretaking style from what the child is used to. This fact alone may directly influence the child's sleep patterns.

A similar study focused on a group of eighty babies and young children whose mothers went to participate in a scientific conference for a few days. For some of the children, the separation was part of an ongoing pattern of frequent separations from the mother, and for others, this was the first significant separation. One of the research questions was whether frequent separations teach the child to cope with separation — and to understand that after a separation comes a reunion — or whether recurring, cumulative separations are stressful situations that hurt the child over and over again, without allowing him to recuperate. The results of the study supported the first hypothesis. For most of the variables that were examined, and also for measures of sleep, the results indicated more significant damage to the group of children that underwent their first significant separation from their mothers. After the separation, these babies spent less time sleeping in general, and particularly deep sleep, and spent more time crying and in distress than before the separation. In this group of babies, sleep returned to its previous pattern immediately upon the mothers' return, and long-term changes in sleep were not observed. For the "experienced" babies, who had undergone several separations in the past, the separation had almost no ramifications based on the measures that were examined.

The changes that took place in sleep patterns of babies during the separation from their mothers due to their hospitalization were different from those that took place when the reason for separation was the mothers' participation in a professional conference. It is unclear why different types of separation have different effects on babies' sleeping patterns. Different psychological aspects are probably related to the ability to prepare the child for separation, the degree of familiarity with the type of separation, the significance of getting a new sibling, and the way in which the parents perceived the event. Whatever the reasons, in both cases a change in the child's sleep patterns was observed as an immediate reaction to separation from the mother.

The emphasis placed on separation anxiety of the baby who is dependent for her physical and psychological existence on her parents often distracts attention from *parents'* significant separation anxieties, especially among mothers. In many cases a mother fears that without her constant supervision, her child will somehow get hurt or be mistreated. This worry and the desire to protect the child and to refrain from deserting him apparently are biologically based and presumably function to ensure the proximity of the mother for her child's survival. We must realize that in many cases the concern and fears get out of hand, overwhelming the mother's cognitive and emotional processes and limiting the mother and child. Exaggerated separation anxiety on the part of the mother can stem from her own history as a neglected or deserted child, from concerns related to the child's special needs (for example, when the child is at risk medically in some way), or from other special circumstances. Some parents who lost children due to illness or accident in early childhood, for instance, tend to develop great anxiety about their subsequent children's health and welfare. Such parents feel that they must watch over their children personally to guard against all potential dangers. These anxieties, whether they are based in any sort of reality or not, may make a parent miserable and may undermine the development of the child's sense of physical and emotional separateness and autonomy. Night separation, of course, is most significant for those parents who often feel that they are deserting the baby for long hours of loneliness and distress. Some parents check many times throughout the night to see whether the baby is "okay." They make sure he's alive, check to see that he's breathing, and so on. This worry, though based on the healthy need to take care of and protect the baby, often makes it hard for parents to allow the baby to go through the night without needing them.

"She won't sleep without her ratty 'blankie'"

Soothing Techniques and Accessories

A child must develop the ability to calm herself and to attain an inner sense of stability in times of distress. She must do this in order to cope with the periodic absence of her soothing and protective parents. This ability is essential for adaptation and mental health. The lack of such an ability is manifested in stressful and anxious situations, particularly among people who suffer from emotional disturbances. One of the salient expressions of the inability to calm oneself, both in childhood and in adulthood, is sleep disturbance. Many adults who have difficulty falling asleep at night report nagging thoughts, fears, anticipation of stressors in day-to-day life, and an inability to "silence the engine," to calm down, and to fall asleep. In many cases, efficient treatment is based on relaxation techniques, self-hypnosis, or other methods that aid people in calming themselves and falling asleep.

The ability to calm oneself is, to a great extent, a learned ability, which the child acquires from her parents. Over the course of early childhood, parents calm their child by reacting to her distress signals and making sure to meet her needs. Guided by these strategies, the child gradually attains a variety of methods to calm herself, and her parents intervene less and less, allowing her to develop the abilities she has acquired to calm herself and to ensure that her needs are met. One of the leading contributors to the understanding of these processes was D. W. Winnicott, a pediatrician who became a child psychologist. Winnicott emphasized that parents' occasional failure to understand, to meet the immediate needs of, and to calm the baby gives the child opportunities to cope with frustrations and to develop her own new abilities. The "good-enough mother," according to Winnicott, is one who tries, and usually succeeds, to understand, to accommodate, and to calm her child. Unlike the unrealistic ideal of the "perfect mother," however, she sometimes fails and frustrates the child, and thus supplies moderate pressure for the child to develop, to withstand frustrations, to delay gratification, and to adopt ways of calming herself.

This developmental process of a child attaining functional and emotional autonomy is not a consecutive and uniform one, and it is laden with many difficulties. The distinguishing point is that a child who is emotionally healthy and received a "secure base" of confidence from her parents will strive to widen her areas of independence and will explore and adopt new patterns of behavior, coping with frustrations and self-calming. Often, however, a child finds herself in stressful situations and is frightened by the independence she has acquired. She may fear that she will lose her parents and the security they have given her if she distances herself from them. In these situations, the child tries to get closer to her parents and expects them to relate to her accordingly. The parents in turn are surprised that the child, who has already shown signs of independence, suddenly "regresses" and reveals renewed dependence.

A typical assumption is that healthy parents naturally fulfill the needs of the baby who is dependent upon them and, with time, accept and support signs of the child's independence. In reality, it is often difficult for parents to accept and to patiently react to the overwhelming dependence of the baby on them; similarly, it is sometimes difficult for them to let go of their child's dependence, and their negative reaction may stifle the buds of the child's independence. A mother might, on the one hand, complain that her child is dependent upon her, wakes her up many times each night, and insists that she calm him and put him back to sleep. On the other hand, the same mother might insist on continuing to comfort the child and to put him to sleep after the child has given signals that he no longer needs parental support. And so the developmental process can be seen as a sort of ongoing negotiation between the child and his parents. The child fluctuates between his interest in widening his range of function and independence and his fears of separation, whereas the parents usually expect the child to develop and adopt new abilities but sometimes fear that they are losing their child when he becomes too independent.

Winnicott claimed that one of the most essential processes that takes place over the course of development is the "transition" of the parental figures and the roles they fulfill from external reality into the inner world of the child. This transition can be described as well in simpler terms of learning and acquiring behavioral patterns that the child "internalizes," or adopts as part of his behavioral repertoire. Winnicott claimed that the transition takes place on two levels, via "transitional objects" and "transitional phenomena." Winnicott's transitional objects are things that the parents offer to the child in order to calm him, or that the child "finds" and adopts on his own. A pacifier, a bottle, a cloth diaper, or a blanket, for instance, might become important for the child in the calming process, and the child learns to use the object to calm himself without the help of others. Winnicott emphasized the importance of these objects as a symbol of transferring "ownership" of calming from the parent to the child.

Transitional phenomena are activities by which the child calms himself. In many cases, these activities were introduced by the parents as calming strategies. One of the most common methods for calming a baby is rocking or rhythmic movement. The mother rocks the child when nursing him, when taking him for a stroll in the carriage, and when he is in the cradle. Some mothers use an automatic device that moves the crib at a steady rhythm in response to the baby's crying, applying the same behavioral pattern employed by mothers to calm many generations of babies. The baby not only enjoys the rhythmic movements that the environment supplies him with, he also learns to elicit them by himself and to use them to calm himself at sleep time. It seems that rhythmic motion is the preferred pattern among many children. Premature babies have been found to enjoy the rhythmic activity of objects in their environment just as full-term babies do (see sidebar).

Rhythmic motion may have such an important role because of the fetus's location in a space that directly transmits its mother's rhythmic movements — her heartbeat and breathing patterns. Studies show that babies have an innate readiness to "look for" their mothers or for stimuli that resemble the human figure, and that the moment they find these stimuli, substantial behavioral and bodily changes take place. It has been found, for example, that babies calm down in reaction to musical notes or vibrations that resemble their mothers' heartbeats or breathing patterns. It has also been found that babies make rhythmic sucking actions (on a pacifier, for exam-

The Adventures of
the Breathing Bear in the Baby's Crib

In one of the original studies in the field of infant sleep and premature babies, Prof. Evelyn Thoman and her colleagues investigated the question of whether babies born prematurely prefer having an object placed in their crib and whether this preference influences their sleep patterns. They placed a small teddy bear in the cribs of the babies in the premature ward. Some of the babies were given a regular soft teddy bear. Other babies were given teddy bears that looked similar to the others but "breathed" via an air pump. It was found that the babies who received a breathing teddy bear had more contact with it over the course of the weeks of the study than did those who received a regular teddy bear. After release from the premature ward, the babies who had been given a breathing teddy bear had more mature sleep patterns when they attained full birth age. In a similar study it was found that the babies who had been in contact with a breathing teddy spent more time in quiet sleep, smiled more during dream sleep, and cried less. These scientists concluded that babies born prematurely are able to regulate their body movements by moving toward and staying in close contact with an object that provides rhythmic stimulation (perhaps reminiscent in certain respects of a mother's body), and that this exposure has a positive influence on maturation and developmental processes.

ple) in response to stress, and that these rhythmic movements (that are unrelated to eating) aid them in calming down. Rhythmic sucking, rhythmic head turning, and other body movements aid the child in calming down and falling asleep, and most children use rhythmic body movements at some stage of their life in the process of falling asleep. Sometimes the rhythmic activity is so intense (fierce shaking of the crib or vigorous head banging against the wall, for example) that it raises concern among parents. Parents are usually advised in these cases to allow the child to use these patterns to fall asleep but to protect him, as needed — for instance, by padding the place where he bangs his head.

In Winnicott's scheme, transitional objects — a pacifier, a bottle, a diaper, a teddy bear, or a piece of a blanket, for example — are key in attaining the ability to calm oneself. And indeed, Isabel Paret found that babies who sleep through the night were more likely to suck their thumbs and use transitional objects. In another study it was reported that 45 percent of four-year-old children used a transitional object, with a linear decrease to 7 percent by age fourteen. Girls tended to use transitional objects more than boys. No correlation was found in this study between the use of transitional objects and characteristics of sleep or night fears.

Abraham Wolf and Betsy Lozoff found a correlation between parental presence with the child while she falls asleep and the use of transitional objects. Children who fell asleep without parental presence tended to use transitional objects more than children who fell asleep with a parent nearby. This correlation also points to the possible role of the transitional object as a mediator in the transition from wakefulness to sleep when the parent doesn't fulfill this role.

The most common transitional phenomenon, em-

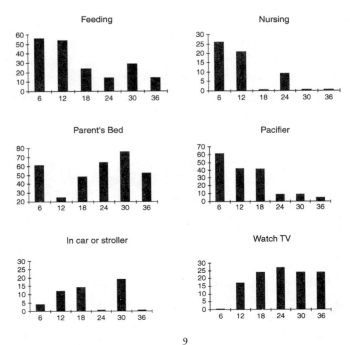

9

Parental use of soothing techniques for baby in daytime and nighttime. The horizontal axes indicate the age of the children in months. The vertical axes indicate percentages of parents who reported using nursing, feeding, a pacifier, taking the child into the parental bed, watching television, and taking a ride in the car or stroller in order to calm the child and cause him to fall asleep.

ployed by almost half of all children, is rhythmic movements of the limbs, the head, or the entire body. Sometimes a behavioral "ritual" of rhythmic movements persists until adulthood and becomes a bothersome and embarrassing sleeping disorder. Both transitional objects and transitional phenomena help the child when she needs to be calmed, especially in the transition to sleep. Although their psychological role is not sufficiently clarified enough in the Wolf and Lozoff study, these strategies illustrate the complexity of the process that helps the child compensate for separation, and calm herself in ways that are directly related to sleep disturbances. The study of Anat Sher and colleagues, which found that 80 percent of babies and young children in an Israeli sample fell asleep while sucking a bottle, a pacifier, or a thumb is illuminating in this context. This percentage, higher than reported in most of the literature, calls into question whether stress and cultural factors unique to the Israeli society are causes that influence the baby's ability to calm herself. Or perhaps this finding is explained by differences in habits concerning caretaking and child-rearing practices.

Many parents who use a sleep watch to examine the baby's sleep report that the watch itself becomes significant for both parents and child. The child sometimes becomes attached to the device and reminds them to put on their watch. Some older children insist on wearing it all the time and taking it to activities outside the home. Many parents half-jokingly suggest that the sleep watch is a treatment factor and that they worry about "withdrawal" from it. These concerns demonstrate that the sleep watch fulfills at least the symbolic function of a transitional object, for the parents as well as the children. In other words, it becomes "something" that keeps the child from being alone when he is in bed and should calm down and fall asleep.

One singular example of self-calming that I came across in the clinic involved a two-year-old boy named Guy. His parents, both doctors, came to the clinic because of their son's manner of falling asleep. For more than six months Guy had fallen asleep while severely shaking his head and banging it against the wall. According to their description, the phenomenon was so severe that their neighbors complained about the knocking against the apartment wall. Although his parents had read about this phenomenon and knew that it was probably normal and would pass with time, they needed a confirming consultation.

During the initial interview the topic of self-calming arose. Guy's parents told me that they have no other way to calm their son. They said that he refuses to use a pacifier or a bottle to calm down and fall asleep. After the interview they were issued a sleep watch for a weeklong home assessment. Arriving at our second meeting, they expressed astonishment. From the first night, once they put the sleep watch on Guy, he fell asleep quietly and every trace of head banging disappeared. The parents told me that their child was fascinated by the sleep watch and enjoyed wearing it on his ankle. Before I could share my thoughts with the parents about the role that the sleep watch fulfilled for Guy, the father told me that the morning before this meeting they had decided to purchase a toy watch and put it on Guy's foot instead of the sleep watch, which they returned to the clinic. In a case like this, of course, it is difficult to evaluate what really caused the immediate disappearance of the stubborn pattern of head banging. Clearly, though, the sleep watch served as a transitional object that accompanied the child when he went to sleep. Its introduction brought about an essential change in his needs for self-calming and fulfilled the role previously served by head banging.

Parents' opportune descriptions cast additional light on the process of "weaning" the child from their active intervention in calming him for the transition stage to sleep. Some parents have reported that they began to hear the child mumble or talk to himself, or rock or develop other rhythmic activities while staying awake alone, often for some time until falling asleep. This strategy is a transitional phenomenon, a behavior that helps the child calm himself and arrive at a state of sleep, in lieu of calming strategies formerly employed by the parents. The phenomenon exemplifies the interaction between the parental decision to wean the child and the child's own flexibility for developing these independent functions. In this way, the child transfers the focus of the parents' regulation to himself and develops the ability to calm down and go to sleep on his own. This ability has a strong correlation with the ability to be alone, which is related to the child's (or adult's) inner feeling that he is secure and not dependent on any other significant person in order to exist emotionally. This ability has great importance in personality development, and significant impairment to it may cause emotional disturbances.

10

"He'll sleep only in our bed"

Communal Sleeping, Separate Sleeping, and
Cultural Outlooks

I encountered an amusing case in the clinic related to communal sleeping, or "cosleeping." A couple came for treatment with their fifth child, who was two years old. They complained that their son insisted on sleeping in their bed with them and that they wanted to stop the practice once and for all. In our discussion, I learned that this couple had a long-standing tradition of allowing their children to sleep with them. The eldest child began the tradition and slept in the parental bed every night. When the second son was born, he joined them in bed. When the third child was born and began to insist on joining the group, the eldest, by this time five years old, agreed to give in and sleep on his own, because the parental bed was not big enough for five. When the fourth child was born and insisted on joining in, the second child moved to his own bed. This was the situation when the fifth child was born, joining the parental bed and pushing out his older brother, the third-eldest child in the family. By this time the parents were at their wit's end for lack of privacy and comfort, and they sought help in "weaning" their children from the long-standing cosleeping tradition. This case illustrates a widespread issue in the field of the development of babies' sleep.

Another cultural tradition exists that is diametrically opposed to this family's routine. This tradition embraces the idea that babies should sleep out of their homes, communally with their peers and away from their parents. This was one of the educational principles of the kibbutz movement, and diverse and strange justifications were made for it. This experiment failed the test of reality, however. Kibbutzniks learned that parents need to be near their baby, and that children need to be near their primary care givers. In the early stages, parents who were unable to bear being cut off from their young children at night left the kibbutz. Later, some exceptions were made that allowed children to sleep at home with parents, and later the principle collapsed entirely. In a study that took advantage of the survival of communal sleeping on one kibbutz that still kept this tradition, scientists from the Technion Sleep Center compared the sleep of babies and young children in their parents' homes to that of children who slept in communal children's houses or in day-care centers. It was found that children who slept in their parents' houses tended to have longer continuous periods of sleep than those in communal sleeping situations on the kibbutz. The Technion researchers found that the kibbutz children's sleep improved greatly after moving to family sleeping arrangements. They concluded that the improvement in the quality of sleep stemmed from the children's feeling of increased security from sleeping with their family.

In the modern Western world, when we think about the sleep of babies, we usually imagine solitary sleep: a baby sleeping in her crib in her own room, separated from her parents. We assume that the baby needs sleep with no interruptions, and there is an emphasis on quiet and on perfect environmental conditions to protect her sleep. Nighttime awakenings are perceived as a problem that requires intervention. In recent years, a number of scientists have questioned these assumptions.

The anthropologist James McKenna, for example, compared cosleeping and solitary sleep in terms of evolution. He observed that in both premodern human societies and the advanced mammals that most resemble us, the baby sleeps next to his mother, who supplies him with warmth and protection. Distancing the baby from the mother is a gradual process that occurs during wakefulness as well as during sleep. McKenna claimed that the newborn baby probably isn't entirely physiologically mature enough to cope with the environment, and therefore the mother helps him to regulate it. The physical closeness of the mother to the baby also helps him maintain body temperature and perhaps also protects him from other anomalous events (see sidebar). Based on his studies, McKenna held that communal sleeping, at least in the first months of life, is normal and desirable.

Other researchers pointed to communal sleeping as a source of different problems. Studies conducted in societies that proscribe communal sleeping suggest a strong relation between communal sleeping and sleep problems among babies and young children. On the other hand, some studies conducted in societies in which communal sleeping is common practice — among the Hispanic population in the United States, for example, or in samples in European countries — showed no relation between this practice and sleep disturbances. It seems that communal sleeping is more likely to be the result of a sleep problem than the source. A child who awakens frequently and has difficulty calming down can drive his parents to despair and to compromise on communal sleeping, even if it is unacceptable to them.

What Does Sleeping with Mother Do for a Baby?

In a series of studies done by the anthropologist and sleep scientist James McKenna and colleagues, communal sleep of babies and their mothers was compared in the sleep clinic with separate sleeping. The researchers found several characteristics that contrast the sleep of the baby who slept with his mother in the first two to four months with that of the baby who slept alone:

- More frequent awakenings accompanied by maternal awakening;
- More transitions between stages of sleep;
- Less time spent in deep sleep;
- Exchange with the mother of gases in the air during the parallel breathing processes.

The researchers claimed that these processes are probably necessary for the baby who is not physiologically mature enough to regulate all bodily functions in the first few months of life, and they raised the possibility that interrupted sleep and limited deep sleep can help prevent crib death. Even though most scientists in the field disagree with McKenna's interpretation of his findings, interest in his work led to the first laboratory study of the sleep patterns of mother and baby dyads.

Another source of growing concern with regard to infant-parent cosleeping is the possibility of suffocation. Recent studies have found a greater suffocation risk for infants sharing a bed with their parents, particularly for babies under four months of age. These risks are related to entrapment under the adult's bodies in a bed not designed for babies. Although these studies stirred professional controversy, parents should take such risk seriously.

From a psychological point of view, communal sleeping often fulfills a mutual need for closeness and security. Many parents tell me about the enjoyment and sense of "pampering" they derive from sleeping next to the baby. These parents feel that they fulfill the baby's needs by giving him maximum security at the same time they calm their own anxieties that arise when they don't have eye contact with the baby. The baby often fills some need as a close "partner." This is especially striking in the stories of the mother who gives in to the baby's demand to sleep with her, particularly when the father is away on business travel or for some other reason. In these situations many mothers admit that they feel more comfortable with the child at night, after having "forgotten" how to sleep alone. When the mother needs to cope with the emotional significance of a temporary separation from her husband, she can find great relief in heightened closeness to the baby, even if it means breaking a family taboo against sleeping with the baby. This phenomenon is also very common among single mothers. In other cases, the baby's presence in the parental bed has a different hidden function, related to a problem in intimacy between the parents. The child's presence can provide an excuse to defer or refrain from intimate relations.

Many parents who come to the sleep clinic have begun to sleep with their children because of sleep problems. These parents may try to stop the practice on the one hand, and use it, on the other, to mollify the child when he refuses to be calmed in any other way. The parents' ambivalence toward this practice conveys a confusing message to the child, who cannot infer a clear expectation about his sleeping. In these situations, the child usually increases his pressure tactics (crying, expression of fears) to persuade his parents to agree to communal sleeping. In the clinic we sometimes have one parent sleep in the child's room as an efficient calming device to solve a sleep problem.

Communal sleeping among older children can present a more serious problem because it usually manifests an agenda of the child's — to assuage fears, for example, or to be near the parents or win exclusivity over his siblings who sleep in their own rooms. Likewise, parents must confront questions of what the child is exposed to when he sleeps in the parental bed, what price the parents pay for his presence in their bed, and what the ramifications are for their intimacy. Sigmund Freud stated that one of the most confusing experiences that a young child may have is to witness his parents having sexual intercourse. He held that children have no way of understanding their parents' behavior in this situation and that their emotional development can be complicated by the impact of the experience. Most parents try not to expose the child to sexual activity. In the clinic, however, I have encountered not a few parents who claim that the child — sometimes nursery school– or school-aged — who sleeps in their bed "does not hear or see anything because he is a heavy sleeper."

There is no clear scientific reason to condemn the communal sleeping of parents with the child in his first year, in families for whom this is a comfortable and desirable arrangement. As the child gets older, separate sleeping or sleeping with siblings should be a goal. In cases of sleep disturbance or the child's insistence on communal sleeping, solving the underlying problem should be preferred to the crutch of communal sleeping, which could exacerbate the problem.

"At night she can scream for hours and her father doesn't hear a thing"

The Father's Role

When Debby and John arrived at our meeting to treat the sleep problem of their one-and-a-half-year-old son, Ron, they were very hostile toward and estranged from each other. Debby claimed that John was not interested at all in Ron's sleep problem and left it to her to wake up at night frequently, when she too has to work and function the next day. John countered that he was incapable of helping, for two main reasons: first, he believed that Debby was the cause of Ron's continual awakening and his insistence that she come to calm him many times throughout the night; and second, his own sleeping was very problematic, and if he were to wake up several times at night, he couldn't function in his sensitive and responsible security job.

My impression was that both parents were intelligent, educated, and sensitive to the child's needs. The hostility between them in terms of treating Ron's sleep problem apparently stemmed from problems in their relationship. The attempt to clarify the sources of this hostility initially led to each one digging in his or her heels and concentrating on the argument surrounding Ron's sleep. I later tried to enlist John into treatment, based on his statement that he knew what should be done and that if things were in his hands the problem would have been solved a long time ago. Although there was logic in John's attitude, Debby continued to oppose it with great hostility, and John was drawn into harsh exchanges of mutual blaming. Finally Debby asserted that when John wanted to spend nights out for his own reasons, he didn't worry about his ability to function at work. Suddenly the picture began to clear up quickly. It turned out that during the course of Debby's pregnancy and the first stages after the birth, John had become involved in a romantic relationship at work. Debby had become aware of the relationship, and the parents had been on the verge of separating. Finally, after difficult deliberation, the father had decided to end the affair, and the couple had decided to continue their life together. A lot of hostility remained between them, however, and each party felt "betrayed" by the other. First, John felt that Debby had lost all interest in him from the moment she became pregnant, making him feel as if he had done his part and was no longer needed. Debby claimed that John had distanced himself, but in any case she had been busy and preoccupied by her feelings and fears about the pregnancy and birth. Treatment helped the parents understand the crisis they had gone through and their important choice to continue living together. In the early stages of treatment John felt that he was able to cope with Ron's sleeping problem, and indeed, after he put Ron to bed for a few nights and dealt with him during the night, the problem disappeared.

The special role of the father is a persistent focus in treating babies' and young children's sleep problems. Our familiarity with the important role of the father has led us always to require his involvement in the treatment process. In many cases, we find that parents have very different perceptions about the baby, his development, and his sleep problems. Parents often come to us with opposite opinions about the right tactic to use in order to solve the child's sleep problem, and a professional can function as a sort of agreed-upon mediator.

The father's role in child development has been neglected for many years in research and in clinical dealings with sleep disturbances. The mother-baby relationship has a special nature: only the mother can carry the baby in her womb and nurse him after birth. Strong societal and cultural conventions still prevail under which the mother is the person primarily responsible for raising the child and the father is responsible for the family's financial security. This relationship has been the subject of much study and a point of emphasis on the clinical treatment of babies and children with developmental disturbances. In recent years, an essential change has taken place with regard to the father's importance in raising the child. Social rewards have led women out of the house and to develop careers. The paternal role and partnership in raising children has come to be generally accepted.

Modern fathers can be divided into types. On one end of the spectrum we find the father who sees himself totally involved in pregnancy, birth, and child rearing. In some cases, these fathers even give up or suspend careers in order to fulfill this role and allow the mothers to continue nurturing their careers. At the other end of the spectrum we find fathers who feel that the role of child rearing belongs to the mother, that they themselves have no ability or inclination to be involved in a substantial way. Many fathers feel that they cannot be involved in early childhood; they prefer to wait until the child "becomes a person," when the father expects the child to become a partner or friend. Most fathers are naturally somewhere along the continuum between these two poles.

The widespread perception today, from a developmental standpoint, is that the father has important roles in his baby's early years. On a practical level, the father can physically help in child rearing, and in doing so, he meets the baby's needs and helps the mother. This physical help can be expressed as ongoing caretaking of the baby — diaper changing, bathing, feeding, calming, and playing — in which many modern fathers feel increasingly willing and able to take part during the day and at night. On an emotional level as well, the father can help both the mother and the baby. As a regular and stable element of the caretaking environment, the father is a source of significant emotional communication and can be an anchor of security for the child. He can also moderate separation anxieties and the storms that exist in the dependent baby-mother relationship. For the mother, the father can be an important source of emotional support and problem solving in raising the child. Because mothers are particularly sensitive in the initial attachment process with the baby, they are apt to find themselves physically exhausted, emotionally vulnerable, and often lonely in confronting the fears and anxieties about the baby and the maternal role. The father can be a moderating, soothing, and helpful influence, and can thus improve the mother's maternal ability.

Through constant presence in the world of the mother and the baby, the father consistently transmits to both that the strong mother-baby tie is not an all-exclusive relationship. He repeatedly reminds them that an outer world exists that makes additional demands. Furthermore, when the mother is impatient, nervous, depressed, or angry with the baby, the father can become involved and moderate the mother's reactions or can take her place until she can regulate and moderate her emotional reactions herself. Each parent brings to the relationship with the baby his or her own inner world, family history, and present-day conflicts and pressures. The child's perception and interpretation of his relationship with each parent can become distorted by these unconscious factors. Sometimes the parents can show each other the distortions in their relationship with the child and can help each other see their own "dark sides" in relation to the baby.

One of the difficult issues for a father who is involved with raising his baby is coping with his own feelings about the mother-baby relationship. Many fathers naturally feel deserted when suddenly the mother devotes all her attention, feelings, and thoughts to the baby. As we saw earlier in this chapter, the father may be deeply jealous of the baby and angry at the mother for deserting him. He may feel that he is trying to penetrate a unique relationship in which he is unwelcome. The mother must help the father feel included, wanted, and significant. Many mothers tend to enjoy their preferred status with the baby and to ignore the father's feelings. This neglect can hurt the parents' relationship and undermine the father's willingness to be involved in child rearing.

In working with parents who seek help for their baby's sleep problems, the initial therapeutic message relayed to the parents is that both of them are perceived as equally valuable and essential factors. Sometimes just getting the father to join the meeting is an important step in improving his involvement in treating the child. In many cases we can turn the father into a main agent of change that can lead to the solution of the child's sleep problem.

Research in the field of sleep disturbances in childhood has not yet been updated with recent changes in the father's role. Even today, many studies point to the mother's role, her emotional status, behavior, and personality in relation to the child's sleep problems. Clinical experience has shown that once the father's role is examined in the same light, his involvement will be found to be a key part in the normal development of the child's sleep patterns.

II
Sleep Disorders

12

"He falls asleep only in the car, and in the middle of the night that's absurd"

Difficulties Putting the Baby to Sleep

ourteen-month-old Richard usually shows signs of tiredness between seven and eight o'clock in the evening. His parents try to put him to bed. He lies in bed for about ten minutes and then stands up and begins to cry and to call them. They wait about ten minutes to see whether he'll calm down and fall asleep. The child continues to cry and refuses to calm down. The mother arrives, takes Richard in her arms and tries to calm him by rocking him. After about fifteen minutes of vigorous rocking, the child calms down and seems to be asleep. The mother returns Richard to his crib. She doesn't even make it out of the room before Richard is standing in his crib and crying. The mother gives up and leaves the room. Richard calms down and continues playing in his crib quietly for about ten minutes and once again renews his shouting cry. Richard's father comes into the room, takes him out of his crib, sits him down in his stroller, and begins to walk him around the house. After about twenty minutes Richard falls asleep. The father waits a while to be sure that he's really sleeping and then lays him in his crib. The child wakes up and the whole process begins anew.

This account of one of the more difficult sleep disturbances I encountered in the sleep clinic describes what happened every night for two to three hours. In addition, the child awoke many times throughout the night. Cases such as this raise the question: why is it so hard for some children (and adults) to go to sleep and to sleep soundly?

Going to sleep is so easy. So it seems to many of us who can't wait to put our heads on our pillows and become engulfed in luxurious sleep. A deeper knowledge of common sleep disturbances among children and adults teaches us that "turning off" from wakefulness and entering into slumber is a complex and vulnerable process that is influenced by many variables. The baby's refusal to go to sleep is usually expressed by protest, anger, and crying. As the process lengthens, the parents become distressed and angry with the stubborn baby, or they hold a lengthy dialogue with her, trying to put her to sleep—which she refuses to do, and so they repeat their attempts, and the vicious cycle continues.

Problems with going to sleep can be divided into a few types. The differences among them are important and may point to both the problem and a possible avenue for treatment. In general, we can differentiate between refusal to go to sleep, which typically has an emotional-behavioral basis, and difficulty falling asleep, which may stem from physiological reasons related to the biological clock.

The first and most common type of difficulty is related to many psychological and familial factors. The child often begins to resist sleep immediately at the start of the rituals that lead up to bedtime. Sometimes the source, as we have seen, is a problem separating from parents. The refusal to lie down and go to sleep may express anxiety related to the coming separation, the need to continue the pleasurable connection with the parents, or anxieties related to nighttime, darkness, and being alone in the dark. In many cases, the parents aren't aware of the intensity of their child's need for the connection and the price they pay for not meeting these needs. One of the most memorable cases I dealt with was of two-year-old Daniel, who refused to go to sleep before ten or eleven o'clock at night, despite showing signs of tiredness much earlier in the evening. It turned out that Daniel's father, an attorney in private practice at the beginning of his career, returned home late each evening, and this was the only time he could devote to playing with and relating to his child. Because it wasn't clear that the relationship with the father was the source of Daniel's trouble falling asleep, we agreed that in order to evaluate the subject, he would attempt to come home earlier during the week before our next meeting. When the father came home earlier in the afternoon, devoted time to his child, and then returned to work, Daniel went to sleep earlier in the evening, with no problems. Daniel's reaction to the change in routine clearly indicated that his problem was related to his basic need to be with his father.

Often a child's fears and stresses are expressed as a difficulty falling asleep rather than a refusal to go to sleep. Problems falling asleep are often related to the absence of the ability to self-soothe — by using a pacifier, for example, or another transitional object or transitional phenomenon. In spite of the parents' natural tendency to intervene and to solve the problem for the child by calming him quickly, it is actually recommended to allow children to find their own solutions, especially if they do not show salient distress signals and problems in trying to fall asleep.

The second type of problem in falling asleep is related

to the biological clock. These difficulties are described clinically, particularly among adults and teenagers. Up until recently, sparse knowledge existed about cases of young children who suffered from them, but more and more of these cases have been reported recently. As we have seen, the biological clock dictates the child's times of fatigue and alertness. In order for the child to be willing to lie down and go to sleep, he needs to get a physiological signal of fatigue. Babies usually show signs of tiredness in the form of eye rubbing, crankiness, crying, and increased agitated activity.

The biological clock, which controls sleep and wakefulness and serves as a mediator between a person's internal rhythm and that of the environment, signals at different times for different people. We often discriminate between "morning types" and "evening types." Evening types are children or adults who tend to go to sleep late and have a hard time waking up in the morning. Morning types become tired in the early hours of the evening, tend to go to sleep early and willingly, and rise early without difficulty.

Disturbances in the timing of sleep are extreme manifestations of the natural tendency reflected in differences between morning types and evening types. The extreme of the evening type will be expressed in a delay in the biological clock, which keeps the child awake in the late evening hours. Contrary to parental expectations, the child shows no signs of tiredness. In other words, this is not a tired baby who is stubbornly "battling" sleep. Rather, he is a child who simply is not yet tired. If we try to put him to sleep at an age-appropriate time, he has difficulty falling asleep. If we wait until later, when the child begins to be tired, he will fall asleep easily and without any special problems. The source of this phenomenon, which is common among both older children and adults, is that the internal clock cycle that regulates sleep and wakefulness tends to be slightly longer than twenty-four hours. The natural tendency is thus to go to sleep later each day. It is easier for most people to stay awake an hour or more past their normal bedtime than to go to sleep an hour earlier than usual. Social and familial temptation related to activity during the late evening hours may exacerbate this type of sleep problem. If parents fail to maintain a clear and consistent sleep schedule, a pattern of time-delayed sleep may arise. Often, even if this tendency began because of environmental-familial causes, it can become a physiological problem that will be very hard to change.

A less common phenomenon among young children, related to the timing of early sleep, is the extreme manifestation of the morning-type pattern. Such a child shows signs of extreme tiredness in the late afternoon or early evening and tends to go to sleep very early, even at the cost of rearranging schedules, meals, and naps. The main difficulty of this phenomenon is early-morning awakening, which demands that parents provide attention and supervision before they have had adequate rest.

The cumulative knowledge about the biological clock teaches us that we can't change it quickly or dramatically, and we must consider the adaptation difficulties involved in changing the clock. Parents who have experienced jet lag with their children know that night suddenly becomes day and day becomes night. Even a healthy baby, child, or adult with consistent sleep patterns usually needs a few days to adapt. Parents who consider their child's sleep time should keep that principle in mind.

Some treatments are based on controlled exposure to light at times appropriate for the character of the child's problem. These treatments are found to be efficient for certain types of biological clock disturbances such as

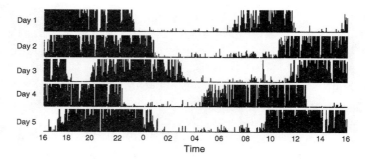

10

Sleep-wake patterns of a three-and-a-half-year-old girl who suffers from a severe developmental delay and from a sleep-schedule
disorder. On the first night she fell asleep around 11 P.M., on the
second night around 1 A.M., and on the third night not until
around 3 A.M. We can see that when she is asleep, her sleep has
no disturbances, and the significant problem is only in the timing
of sleep.

those described in figure 10. But less clinical strategies can
be successful in mild cases. If the child falls asleep every
night at eleven o'clock, and the parents want him to fall
asleep at nine, they should try advancing bedtime gradually, over a long period of time. They might try to have
bedtime a half-hour earlier for a week or two or longer,
until the child adapts to this new schedule, then advance
bedtime another half-hour, repeating until the desired
bedtime has been established. Gradually pushing back the
clock for an early riser can be done the same way. Abrupt
attempts to influence bedtime by making it later or earlier
will not influence the biological clock. Worse, such an
approach may trigger more severe sleep problems.

13

"She awakens every hour on the hour"

Nocturnal Wake-Up Calls

The parents of one-year-old Mark put him to sleep each evening at eight o'clock. The process of putting him to sleep is accomplished very quickly: one of the parents gives Mark a bottle, feeding him until he falls asleep. Then Mark is put into his crib. After about two hours, Mark wakes up. One of his parents, usually his mother, takes him out of his crib and gives him another bottle while holding him. This wakeful state continues about ten minutes, and then Mark is returned to his crib. If the parents refuse to take Mark out of his crib and feed him, he cries and protests vigorously until they respond. Throughout the night Mark wakes up between five and seven additional times, and the process repeats itself, often with longer periods of wakefulness. This pattern of many or lengthy awakenings is the most common complaint in the first two years of a child's life. The child often doesn't appear to suffer from lack of sleep despite the phenomenon, but the parents certainly do.

Unlike Mark, two-year-old Steve wakes up only two or three times a night. Steve's nocturnal awakenings often last one to two hours. Steve is very

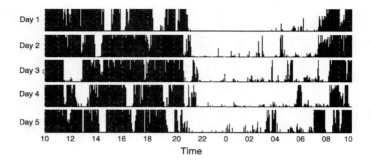

11

The sleep of "angels": a recording of a baby who sleeps very well
and calmly, aside from one nocturnal awakening.

quiet at these times; he entertains himself with the toys
in his crib until he falls asleep again. He is fatigued in the
morning when he is awakened to go to preschool, but his
parents, who are usually not bothered during the night,
are unaware of his sleep problem and suffer none of the
distress experienced by Mark's parents. Steve's lengthy
awakenings were identified by a sleep watch.

Frequent awakenings during infancy are a common
and normal phenomenon. The knowledge in this field is
based on surveys that rely on parents' reports and on
research studies that employ such devices as the sleep
watch, nightly recording, and video filming in the children's homes or in the laboratory. Anat Sher and colleagues of Haifa University's School of Education, for example, conducted a survey in well mother and baby
clinics in Israel. The survey included 661 children from
four months to four years old. Parents reported that 28
percent of the children woke up regularly at least once a
week. In a survey conducted in the United States, Merle
Johnson reported that approximately 35 percent of the
infants and toddlers were defined by their parents has
having a night-waking problem. These percentages range

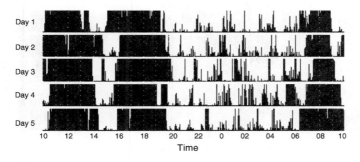

12

The sleep of the "night-shift" baby: a recording of a baby whose sleep is disturbed by frequent nocturnal awakenings, some of which are brief and others longer.

between 20 and 30 percent in other surveys in the United States and other countries.

In a different study in which a sleep watch was used, we examined the sleep of babies nine to twenty-four months old, some of whom were described as good sleepers and others who were referred for treatment in the sleep laboratory. We found that the "good sleepers" woke up on the average of twice a night, every night, and the "problem sleepers" woke up on an average of four times a night. In addition to waking up more frequently, the poor sleepers also summoned their parents each time by crying, calling out, and otherwise protesting. On the other hand, the good sleepers often resumed sleep with no assistance and did not signal their parents when they woke up. Their parents were not aware of many of their nocturnal awakenings.

As the examples of Mark and Steve demonstrate, it is important to differentiate between awakenings that are reported by parents and awakenings that occur without the awareness of the parents. Parents can report only those awakenings that are brought to their attention, usu-

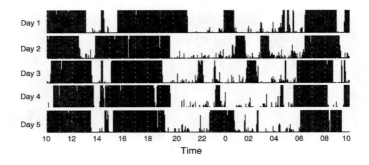

13

An example of a baby whose sleep is disturbed at night by a
small number of awakenings, some of which are very long.

ally when the baby cries or calls out from her crib, or
when an older child gets out of bed and comes to the
parents' bed. Studies show a sizable difference between
parental reports and objective recordings of nocturnal
awakenings among children. When distress signals from
the child establish parental awareness and intervention,
nocturnal awakening is much more likely to be identified
as a sleep problem. But awakenings that go unnoticed by
parents also disrupt the sleep of the child, who may pay
a price for them in her daytime functioning.

The frequency of nocturnal awakenings, both as reported and as documented by objective methods, lessens
with age. It is clear today from recent studies, however,
that the decrease in the actual number of awakenings is
less than was indicated by studies based on parental reports. Researchers have learned that as a child get older,
she becomes less likely to demand parental attention; in
many cases the parents do not even know that the child
has awakened several times in the night. In one study of
normal school-age children we documented an average of
two night wakings per night using the sleep watch. Most

of these night wakings were not reported by the parents or the children themselves.

Frequent nocturnal awakening causes distress primarily to parents, and it is their foremost complaint when they seek treatment for their children. But the baby who wakes up ten times at night usually does so according to his internal clock and in accordance with his sleep cycles. Each time he moves from deep sleep to light sleep, he wakes up and wakes his parents. For the baby, the cost of these awakenings is limited because he falls back to sleep afterward and fulfills his sleep needs. In contrast, parents pay a higher price for the baby's nocturnal awakenings. These episodes are usually not coordinated with the internal clocks of the parents, who therefore awaken from the depths of sleep and suffer damage to the quality of their sleep. Likewise, in most cases, the parent cannot compensate effectively for lost sleep because of work and family constraints. For these reasons, parents who seek help for the problem of frequent nighttime awakenings are often exhausted and feel helpless.

There are many potential causes for nocturnal awakenings in infancy. They can be caused by physical discomfort resulting from teething, hunger, sickness, or inappropriate environmental conditions (noise, temperature, bedding material). Emotional needs and behavioral patterns play an important role in night wakings. A baby who wakes up often but just requires a brief parental intervention might be checking on her parents to make sure they are around and available — a basic necessity for her sense of security. Clinical research and practice suggest that often nocturnal awakenings have become a behavioral pattern because they are rewarded by the parents (with sweet drinks, maternal attention, or a chance to join the parents in bed). It is difficult for parents to understand how a baby can "intentionally" wake up to collect these "prizes," but our sleep is very sensitive to our motivation and expectations. For instance, most of us can recall experiences of waking up several times at night to check whether the alarm clock has failed to rouse us for an important meeting or a scheduled flight. This heightened sensitivity to special circumstances is probably more typical in infancy.

Regardless of the cause of the night wakings, parents should remember that one or two brief wakings a night are common for most babies and should not be treated as a problem. If night wakings are more frequent or extend in duration beyond the first six months, then an evaluation and intervention should be considered.

14

"He wakes up terribly frightened and doesn't calm down"

Nightmares, Night Terrors, and Other Sleep-Time Phenomena

One night when one of my daughters was ten months old, we heard a terrible scream, accompanied by bitter crying, coming from her room. The forceful scream and the tone of her crying testified that something terrible had happened. Our first thought, as we hurried to her room, was that she had become trapped in the crib slats or suffered some other sudden painful shock. We were surprised to find her sitting in her crib, eyes closed, crying terribly, covered with sweat. To our surprise, when we tried to pick her up and pacify her, not only did she not calm down, but the opposite occurred: she began to kick us and resist our attempts to hold her, vigorously crying in the highest tone possible but with her eyes still shut. Finally we switched on the light and washed her face with water. She then woke up, calmed down, and appeared to be totally unaware of what had happened just moments before. In a matter of seconds, she fell back to sleep in her crib.

This phenomenon, called night terror, is one that may frighten parents who come face to face with it for the first time without having heard of it before. It is characterized by partial awakening accompanied by crying or other extreme expressions of distress. The child is typically unaware of his surroundings and does not welcome or relate to parental attempts to calm him down. Night terrors appear during the first year of life and usually disappear as the child grows. It is important to understand that this is a normal phenomenon and that episodes are common but isolated events among many babies and young children. When parents encounter night terrors in their young child, they must understand that even though it looks like the child is going through a terrible experience, he will awaken with no memory of the event and calm down quickly without sustaining, as far as we know, any negative effects. In most cases, when the parents wait, the terror subsides by itself in a few minutes and the child calms down and continues sleeping. If the episode continues more than ten minutes, the parents can wake the child and, once he calms down, put him back to bed and let him fall asleep again. It is important not to develop rituals and exaggerated anxieties in response to the event and not to interrogate the child after it or the following morning. Overreacting to the event may encourage repetition, conditioning the child to exploit the secondary benefits of increased parental attention.

It is important to recognize that this phenomenon is influenced by insufficient sleep and by stressful situations involving the child. If the night terrors become frequent and stubborn and do not show signs of letting up, the parents should seek a more thorough evaluation of the problem. An evaluation of this sort can lead to recommendations for changes in the child's sleeping patterns, to clarification and treatment of the sources of stress in the child's life, or to other solutions. For example, a unique intervention is appropriate when night terrors appear frequently at a set time of night. In such cases, the parents can, for a period of one week, wake the child a half-hour before the event is expected, then immediately let him go back to sleep. This strategy is intended to disrupt the child's internal clock, which regulates this phenomenon to a particular time or stage of the sleep cycle. Often this regimen solves the problem.

It is important to distinguish between night terrors and nightmares, which are frightening dreams that cause the baby or child to awake in a state of fear. A child who has already acquired verbal ability can tell us about the scary dream content or about something else that is frightening him greatly (for instance, a monster hiding in the closet). Because young children have trouble distinguishing between a dream and imagination while awake, they cannot always tell the difference between something they dreamed and something they "saw" (in their imagination or in reality) during wakefulness. Whether or not the child is verbal and can report what he experienced, he will be immediately responsive to parental attempts to calm him, and it will be clear that he is awake and attentive to the environment. Occasional nightmares, too, are entirely normal phenomena at all stages of life. Some children from three to five years of age have frequent nightmares and an accompanying rise in fears. At this age, the child is still unable to clearly distinguish between his internal world, the creations of his imagination, the fruits of the imagination of others (books and movies, for example), and shared reality.

In coping with nightmares, parents should calm their child as much as needed. It is important to signal the child quickly that there is no danger and that she can overcome the disturbance and resume her sleep. Sometimes the parents detour from regular patterns, either allowing the child to sleep in their bed or lying next to the child in order to calm her. It is important to return quickly to the routine and to hint to the child that she can cope and will not gain attention or other benefits by exploiting her fears. It is also recommended that parents not interrogate the child about her nightmares during the day. All exaggerated attention may worsen the phenomenon. If a young child has frequent severe nightmares and does not show signs of improvement over time, the parents should seek professional evaluation, because nightmares may stem from anxiety and stress that the child is experiencing.

As we have seen, nightmares and night terrors usually subside as the child approaches elementary school age. Similarly, such phenomena as sleep talking, sleepwalking, and teeth grinding, which are associated with sleep disturbances, begin in early childhood and can disappear later on or accompany the child into maturity. Some would include bedwetting in this category.

Sleep talking can be either mumbling or clear articulation by the sleeping child, who is typically unaware of talking and doesn't remember anything afterward. Laboratory examinations have shown that sleep talking is not related to a particular stage of sleep and is not necessarily part of dream-sleep. Sleepwalking is a phenomenon that has many forms of expression. In some cases it can be manifest as the child's simply sitting up in bed and seeming confused. In other cases, the child roams the house; sometimes he is found later, sleeping in another room or engaging in unusual behavior. An estimated 5–15 percent of all children experience this phenomenon. As isolated events, sleep talking and sleepwalking are most common in early childhood, and these events should not be regarded as worrisome. Although the phenomena seem strange, they appear in early childhood and usually disappear at adolescence or just before, though some cases have continued through maturity. A less common phenomenon is teeth grinding, which often is so intense as to be audible and to damage the protective enamel of the teeth.

The causes of these sleep phenomena are unknown, though they presumably involve a failure in the systems responsible for the transition from the state of sleep to wakefulness or of the systems that are responsible for the suppression of movement during sleep. In such phenomena as sleep talking or sleepwalking, we see a lack of coordination between behavioral systems. Certain systems work during sleep as if the child were awake. Thus the child who walks in his sleep makes his way around the house and exercises significant control over events around him, typically avoiding accidents that would result from bumping into objects, for example. Nonetheless, the child's awareness of his situation is limited, and often he concludes his journey in an illogical destination, with no memory of how he got there. As an interesting and alarming footnote, I will point out that some adults who sleepwalk have succeeded in carrying out complex actions, even driving to a familiar location.

These phenomena are normal during childhood and do not point to any type of medical or emotional disorder. On the other hand, these phenomena occur most frequently and most disruptively in children who suffer from mild or severe neurological disorders that affect mental functioning, bodily control, and movement. Presumably this relation stems from some aberration of the brain's control mechanisms that are related both to the sleep-related phenomena and to neurological disorders.

All the sleep phenomena discussed in this chapter are exaggerated by stressful situations and insufficient sleep. If the phenomenon occurs frequently and doesn't show signs of spontaneous recovery, parents should seek professional evaluation and treatment. Likewise, if any danger is involved, coping strategies must be considered. A child who grinds his teeth, for example, might be seen by a specialist who can offer protection from tooth erosion, and a sleepwalking child must be shielded from potential injury.

15

"She doesn't eat enough, she's teething"

Physiological Factors That Influence Sleep

S leep difficulties in infancy are so common that it is easy to understand how various myths about factors that influence sleep arose. Often these explanations contain a kernel of truth, but the factors are usually given exaggerated importance.

Is There a Relation Between Nutrition and Sleep?

Some of the central topics that parents focus on involve nutrition and breast-feeding, and how they relate to the child's physical development. In the first months, when the baby's weight is being continually charted, one of the basic, traditional parental roles is to feed the baby well in order that he grow and be healthy. Many mothers "measure" their maternal competence according to their degree of success in feeding the baby and the rate of his physical growth. In addition, because the baby is being monitored over the course of his early development, parents often feel as if they too are being evaluated for their success in child rearing. Attention to the baby's nutrition has not just physiological implications for the baby but also psychological implications for parents, especially mothers.

Such subjects as breast-feeding versus formula, the value of nutritional supplements, and feeding on schedule versus feeding on baby's demand are charged debates for both mother and child. In the first months, the baby needs to be fed often and demands as much, at night as well as during the day. It has been found that among three-month-old babies, nocturnal awakenings were directly related to nutrition and to physical discomfort. And so, as many parents assume, at very young ages, when the primary need is to maintain body temperature and satiety, and to minimize stress from pain, the awakenings signal bodily distress.

Gradually, as the child grows and begins to sleep throughout the night, night feedings become less frequent or are discontinued altogether, and the child eats during the daytime hours only. In a study that examined whether the amount of food that four-week-old and four-month-old babies eat influences their sleep, some babies were given regular porridge and others were given porridge with a nutritional supplement before bedtime. The study's findings did not establish any influence of the fortified porridge on the children's sleep. Likewise, other studies did not find a correlation between the amounts of food ingested by the baby and nighttime sleep problems. Insufficient food or "hunger" is not a common cause of sleep problems in healthy infants, except in extreme cases of real malnutrition.

No differences were found for nocturnal awakenings between children who ate on demand and those who ate on schedule. But babies who were nourished according to variable and inconsistent eating patterns were more likely to suffer from chronic night-waking problems during their first year. It appears that lack of consistency in feeding style may reflect general lack of consistency in parental behavior patterns, which may disturb the development and consolidation of normal sleep-wake patterns.

Other studies examined the influences of breast-feeding and formula, though the nature of the two styles makes comparison problematic. Nursing mothers and those who use formula tend to differ not only in the content and packaging of the food they provide but also in the different personal characteristics that influenced their decision whether to breast-feed and if so, for how long.

Longitudinal studies confirm that a relation exists between the length of the breast-feeding period and the on-going problem of nocturnal awakenings. The immediate cause is not behavioral, related to the mothers' decision to nurse until a later age in order to calm their children when they awoke, but the opposite: babies awoke more for a physiological reason that was somehow related to breast-feeding. The researchers suggested that the reason may be that mother's milk remains in the intestines for less time and that the awakenings occur as a result of hunger. Another relation between type of food and sleep was found among children who are allergic to cow's-milk products, who may suffer from stubborn sleep disturbances because of the allergy. This phenomenon was found among children who had ongoing sleep difficulties and did not respond to behavioral treatment. When they were kept on a strict diet of milk substitutes, the problem was solved.

The decision to breast-feed or bottle-feed has many meanings for the mother and the baby beyond direct nutritional needs. The issue of nursing has also significant implications as to the father's involvement because fathers cannot nurse.

"Addicted" Babies

It has become clear that many babies who are under the influence of harmful substances before they are born are physiologically addicted to these substances. A mother who uses drugs or alcohol during her pregnancy hurts the developing child in many ways that may have chronic adverse influences after birth. A breast-feeding mother who uses drugs or alcohol after the birth poisons her baby with the same destructive substances that she uses. Research in this area demonstrates that babies are particularly vulnerable to the influence of these substances. Their neurological development is harmed, and their sleep patterns are influenced for the worse. When one tries to stop the supply of the substances to an addicted baby, her body's physiological response is often manifested as a difficult and painful withdrawal process. Some of the damage done to the central nervous system during its early maturation is irreversible.

Common Illnesses and Phenomena

Common illnesses can have the most essential influence on the baby's sleep patterns. Every cold, runny nose, or flu that causes an excess of fluids and blockages in the respiratory pathways can lead to significant sleep difficulties. Difficulty breathing interferes with the baby's ability to fall asleep or stay asleep. Ear infections and an accompanying accumulation of fluid in the ear can cause the supine baby heightened pain resulting in significant sleep difficulties. Because these problems are intensified when the baby lies down, he often will not show distress signs when awake. In addition to treating infections with medication, parents can often help the suffering baby sleep by adjusting the mattress so that his head is elevated above his body.

Colic, stomach pain that occurs among babies in their first year, can also lead to significant sleep difficulties. Babies who suffer from these pains tend to have lengthy and severe crying attacks. This crying is frequently accompanied by contortions and stiffening of the body. This phenomenon is typically at its worst at age three or four months and usually disappears by the child's first birthday. Various studies show that babies who suffer from heightened pain and crying in early childhood tend also to suffer from sleep disturbances, both during the painful period and later, after the heightened pain and crying have passed. Because colic has many sources that are not well understood, treatment is complex and is, to a great degree, based on trial and error until a way is found to calm the baby. Treatment can include special diets, enforcement of body postures that soothe the baby, burping the baby after meals and, if needed, calming medications.

An additional problem that can cause sleep disturbances is gastroesophageal reflux. This disturbance of the esophageal valve, which ordinarily prevents gastric acids from rising, causes spitting up. Babies who suffer severely from this painful phenomenon can vomit so much food that their development is hampered. Because this phenomenon often worsens when the baby lies down, it may disrupt sleep. The overwhelming majority of babies who suffer from gastroesophageal reflux outgrow the condition during the first years of life. Treatment is based on regulating quantities and content of food, and in severe cases administration of medication. The most important recommendation for avoiding sleep disruption is to make sure that the child lies in an inclined position, with her head higher than her body.

Another development that is notorious for disrupting

a child's sleep is teething. The emergence of teeth from the gums is sometimes accompanied by increased salivation, sucking, gum rubbing, and irritability. Sometimes chewing hard objects eases the baby's distress. A recent large study by Michael Macknin and colleagues found that various symptoms, including night waking, are associated with teething in some infants, though fewer than 20 percent of the sample. The study suggested that there is an eight-day period around the tooth emergence when symptoms are likely to occur. Therefore, even though teething is often used to explain the baby's sleep problems, this explanation could actually be valid only periodically in some of babies. Except for babies who display substantial distress related to the mouth area during the day as well as at night, there is no reason to assume that teething is a cause of ongoing sleep disturbance.

I often see parents who come to our sleep clinic when their child is two years or older. They all tell a similar story, with different variations: During the first six months we thought our child kept waking up because he was breast-fed frequently; during the next twelve months we thought he was waking up because he was teething and suffering frequent ear infections. Later we believed he kept waking up because he was not eating enough during the day. We are here now because we have run out of explanations.

My experience has led me to the conclusion that parents should examine all these potential physical problems and consult their pediatrician. If they complete an evaluation and no direct problem has been identified, there is no reason to attribute the sleep problem to any of these factors. A separate evaluation and intervention for the sleep problem should be able to resolve it expeditiously.

16

"He suddenly stops breathing and it takes my *breath away!"*

Sleep Apnea and Breathing Disorders

One of the most unpleasant experiences for parents when watching their baby sleep is to see her suddenly stop breathing for a long period of time. Finally, after a sudden lurch or a brief awakening, the baby continues to breathe and sleep as if nothing happened. Sometimes this type of event recurs dozens, even hundreds of times during the night. There is a wide range of events related to sleep apnea, some of which are normal, occurring among many babies and disappearing with time. Others are serious and significant and require immediate assessment and treatment.

A baby's sleep disturbances are sometimes hidden from the parents. Certain sleep disturbances can harm the child, severely damaging the quality of his sleep and leading to many other negative consequences. The most common and problematic sleep disturbances are caused by sleep apnea, the failure of the respiratory system during sleep. Interruptions in breathing during sleep occur among babies, especially ones born prematurely, in their first weeks. This phenomenon usually disappears quickly and is not considered a severe disorder. Shorter nonbreathing episodes — called respiratory pauses, lasting a few seconds — are also normal in infants. When the problem is persistent and severe, however, a proper assessment and appropriate treatment are essential.

When we are awake, we typically breathe automatically and do not pay attention to the breathing process. At the same time, we have some control over breathing in the wakeful state. We can stop breathing for a limited period of time and then begin again. We can control our breathing and coordinate it with speech — taking breaths, for example, only at natural pauses in a sentence. When we sleep, the respiratory system becomes entirely automatic. If we stop breathing for some reason, or if insufficient oxygen reaches the brain, a survival mechanism wakes us so that we can resume breathing. As we have seen, every flu or cold that is accompanied by a stuffy nose and a clogged respiratory pathway can disturb sleep by disrupting breathing. These conditions are temporary disturbances that end after a few days, but some illnesses or chronic disorders of the respiratory system require long-term treatment or surgical intervention to remove the source of the disturbance.

Sleep apnea usually results from structural blockages in the respiratory pathways, but it can also stem from aberrations in the nervous system, which regulates breathing. Among children, blockages usually result from enlarged adenoids or tonsils, or from other defects of the pharynx and the respiratory pathways. Many children who suffer from these problems snore and sweat excessively in their sleep. They sometimes also suffer while awake from difficult, heavy, or noisy breathing. Structural defects of the pharynx or difficulty breathing from other causes may also complicate the child's development of normal speech. A typical child who suffers from breathing disturbances stops breathing for a few seconds in the night, wakes up for a brief time, and then goes back to sleep. In severe cases the child might awaken hundreds of times throughout the night, damaging the quality of his sleep significantly. He might be unable to reach the stages of deep sleep at all. Because the awakenings are extremely brief and the child does not become fully awake, in most cases he is unaware of these awakenings and does not call for his parents — and thus they too may remain ignorant of his condition.

The condition may be difficult for the parents to detect. A child who suffers from a severe breathing disorder during sleep is often very tired during the day, willingly napping for extended periods, but parents may interpret those tendencies positively. If they don't become aware of the apnea and don't seek clarification, they may have the false impression that their baby simply sleeps like an angel. The quality of his sleep, however, may actually be much poorer than that of a baby who wakes up several times a night, wakes his parents, asks for a pacifier, and goes back to sleep. In the most severe cases, this type of sleep disturbance may undermine the physical and intellectual development of the child.

Treatment of apnea depends on the type of disturbance and its causes. In the first stage, the problem, its severity, and its exact sources must be fully clarified. This type of assessment requires a full laboratory examination in which respiratory system function is evaluated during sleep. In many cases, blockages exist in the respiratory pathways because of irregularities in the structure of the pharynx or other areas of the "pipelines." Sometimes the child's physical development brings anatomical changes that solve the problem without additional intervention. In other cases — including the common condition of enlarged adenoids or tonsils — surgical intervention can solve the problem.

A modern method used to postpone surgery or make it unnecessary uses a small air compressor connected to a mask attached to the sleeping child's face. Pressurized air flows in through the device to circumvent the respiratory pathway blockages. This type of treatment does not solve the cause of the problem, but it allows the baby or child who can adapt to the mask to sleep well and avoid the drawbacks of severely disrupted sleep.

When parents suspect that their child suffers from chronic respiratory difficulties while sleeping, or when their child suffers from inexplicable excessive fatigue despite seeming to sleep a reasonable amount of time, they must seek out an expert assessment and advice to clarify whether the child does indeed suffer from sleep apnea. If the parents know that the child has enlarged adenoids or tonsils or some other condition that blocks his breathing, they should consider a comprehensive sleep examination to assess the severity of the problem before opting for surgical intervention. In cases of severe apnea that cause parents to fear for the life of the baby, an ongoing assessment of the baby's breathing in his crib should be done.

Milder breathing disturbances may also have negative ramifications on the baby's and child's sleep. One of the most common childhood conditions is asthma. Studies show that between 5 percent and 15 percent of all children suffer from asthma in varying degrees of severity. The physiological and psychological causes and influences of asthma are not clear enough. Asthma is expressed by attacks of shortness of breath, and extreme cases may be life-threatening and require emergency care. Medication usually prevents severe attacks. Asthma attacks are often seasonal and worsen as the season changes. They are often related to allergic reactions that sometimes can be identified and prevented. Likewise, the attacks worsen in stressful and anxiety-producing situations. In sleep, automatic respiratory system functions are vulnerable to asthma attacks that severely damage sleep. Studies have shown a high frequency of sleep disturbances among children who suffer from asthma. In a recent study on school-aged children, my colleagues and I found that the quality of asthmatic children's sleep was lower than that of children in the control group, even though the asthmatic children were taking medication and were in stable clinical condition with no attacks. In addition, these asthmatic children reported increased daytime sleepiness and reduced alertness compared with healthy children.

Of all the sleep problems discussed in this book, those related to breathing problems are potentially the most evasive and dangerous. They are evasive because often parents are unaware of them, simply considering the child a good sleeper. They are dangerous because they can disrupt sleep to the point of having a serious impact on the child's ability to function, on her physical growth, even on her health. Because breathing-related problems in infants and young children are not easy to treat, treatment is sometimes deferred. But it is of utmost importance to detect and diagnose these problems early because of their implications for the developing child.

17

"While she slept we took turns standing guard to make sure she was breathing"

Crib Death, or Sudden Infant Death Syndrome

I t is hard to imagine a more frightening nightmare for a parent than getting up in the morning and finding a lifeless baby in her crib. In the past, infant mortality was a much more widespread phenomenon because of the inability to cope with infectious diseases and with complications during pregnancy and childbirth. Today, with developments in medicine and technology, the infant death rate has decreased dramatically. Nonetheless, SIDS (sudden infant death syndrome) has remained an unsolved mystery to this day and still causes the deaths of babies despite relentless research efforts to understand and prevent it.

"Crib death" is thought to be the primary cause of infant mortality in the first year of life in industrialized countries. The death usually occurs at night while the baby is asleep. The baby is found dead with no comprehensible explanation, even after a thorough examination and autopsy. The incidence of crib death varies from country to country and is affected by many variables that are, it seems, cultural or climatic. In most Western developed countries, the numbers reported range from one to two victims out of every thousand babies. In some countries, however, the frequency reported is close to 1 percent of all babies.

Hundreds of studies have been conducted in an attempt to solve this mystery, but there is still more unknown than known. Several characteristics have been identified in the past few years as risk factors. Crib death is more common among babies who were born prematurely (before week 37 of pregnancy). Likewise, the phenomenon is more common during the winter than any other season of the year. Some studies point to a higher risk among babies of mothers who smoke or are addicted to drugs. The probability for crib death is higher among babies from families in which a baby has previously died of similar causes, with young mothers, and with mothers who have gone through many births. The phenomenon is more frequent among boys, and among families of low socioeconomic level.

Studies have shown that defective functioning of the elements of the nervous system that control breathing, temperature regulation, heart rate, and the mechanism for awakening from sleep may be implicated in crib death. Other evidence suggests that overheating of the environment where the baby sleeps may increase the risk.

An additional assumption is that crib death stems from a failure of the baby's self-survival mechanism. Normally, when respiratory distress occurs, whether due to apnea or to a blockage in the respiratory tract, mechanisms in the brain identify the decrease in oxygen reaching the brain and cause the baby to awaken to resume his breathing. Some evidence suggests that babies who are considered to be at risk for crib death have a higher awakening threshold in response to external stimuli. In other words, compared with normal babies, these babies need a stronger stimulus to wake them. Some researchers believe that this characteristic is related to the failure of these babies to awaken from a state of respiratory distress.

Laboratory studies of the sleep of babies considered at high risk or those who have undergone dangerous but nonfatal respiratory events teach us that the maturation of sleep patterns of these babies is somewhat delayed in comparison to control babies.

One of the research breakthroughs that has recently been cited is the clear and primary finding of a relation between crib death and the baby's sleeping position. Studies have shown that the risk for crib death is up to ten times higher among babies who sleep on their stomachs than for those who sleep on their backs or on their sides. In many countries, this finding has led to the publication of an official recommendation by leading health agencies to put babies to sleep on their backs or on their sides and not on their stomachs. A striking decline in cases of inexplicable death was found in countries in which this recommendation was implemented. A recent review by a task force of the American Academy of Pediatrics indicated that since 1992, when the "back to sleep" campaign started, the number of infants sleeping on their tummy has decreased from more than 70 percent to about 20 percent, and the rate of sudden infant death syndrome has decreased by more than 40 percent. Soft sleep surfaces, soft objects, and loose bedding are additional risk factors that should be avoided.

Over the course of the first few months, many babies suffer from sleep apnea, and some experience events defined as apparent life-threatening events. These are characterized by lengthy apnea, choking, and turning blue. Even though their likelihood of crib death is very low, they are considered to be at high risk. In these cases, doctors often recommend that parents use an alarm to monitor the child's breathing while asleep. This alarm detects an incident of apnea and awakens the child so that he resumes breathing, and also awakens the parents so that they can assist the child. It must be remembered that not all cases can be helped even if they are directly observed. Crib death sometimes occurs when adults are present, and they are unable to stop the event or to change its tragic outcome. Some experts question the use of apnea monitors, which have become popular. These critics believe that the effectiveness of these monitors is questionable in low-risk children and that false alarms may lead to unnecessary medical procedures that carry their own risks.

My introduction to the subject, which etched a deep impression on my memory, came when parents brought their nine-year-old son Nathan to the clinic for treatment of behavior problems. They told me that their first-born son had died from crib death when he was four months old. This death left them shocked, grieving, and broken. A few months later, they decided to have another child. They agreed that during the first year they would take turns guarding their child whenever he slept in order to ensure that he was breathing and alive. Their deep fear of losing their second child and their high level of anxiety led them to relate to their child in an anxious manner. For the first few years, for instance, the mother had great difficulty leaving Nathan with a caretaker or babysitter. The parents gave up any notion of going out without their son. They were anxious any time he had the slightest symptom of illness. These patterns apparently led to the behavior problems for which they sought help. Nathan picked up on the deep parental anxiety about his health throughout his childhood, and he reacted at first by expressing his own anxiety. His behavior became more and more aggressive toward his parents, who could not understand why their child reacted to their great concern with such angry outbursts.

The psychological ramifications of the terrible trauma of the apparently random loss of a child are long-lasting and often find their expression in the relationship with children born subsequently. Prof. Shimshon Rubin of the Department of Psychology at Haifa University has studied these ramifications and found several predictive characteristics. First, in the absence of a clear medical reason for the baby's death, parents tend to manufacture an array of reasons and explanations. Some parents associate between the death and various unrelated factors—the child's name, for example, or the mother's postpartum depression, or the child's bedroom. This pattern is characteristic of the grieving process. It often leads to severe feelings of guilt that are based on the parents' irrational belief that had they acted in a different way—choosing a different name for the baby, or having him sleep in a different room—the death might have been prevented. This guilt and the pain associated with it lead parents to a sense that such events can be controlled or prevented. That belief is probably psychologically preferable to the feeling of helplessness and lack of control that parents often feel after experiencing such a traumatic event that is so unexpected, unpredictable, and unavoidable.

Second, the emotional tie to the child who is born immediately after the sudden death of a child is incomplete until the second child passes the age at which the first child died. It seems that parents have difficulty developing an emotional tie to the next child out of the fear of another difficult, painful, additional loss. This fear is prominent and real for the parents, even though the statistical chance that the phenomenon will occur again is extremely low. It is understandable that these difficulties in emotionally bonding with the child carry a developmental and psychological price for both the subsequent child and the parents. The parents may not be sensitive and responsive to the child's needs, and their emotional reactions to him may become distorted in the wake of their anxieties and unresolved sense of loss.

Third, parents who have lost a baby to crib death tend to have a high level of anxiety and fear for the health of the next child. Likewise, losing a child causes the parents emotional burn-out, which makes it harder for them to function as parents to other children and can cause problems in the family's functioning.

Finally, parents who have lost a baby under these circumstances often idealize the dead child, remembering him in an unrealistically positive light. This response expresses their difficulty in making peace with their loss. As a result, they sometimes see the subsequent child as a substitute; they can't accept him as he is or respond to him in accordance with his own personality and uniqueness. Parental inability to relate to the child for himself may make it harder for the child to develop a sense of self-identity.

The threat of crib death causes many parents to lose sleep from fear that their child will be a victim of this phenomenon. Laboratory tests and sophisticated home equipment are offered to parents around the world in order to assess, identify risk, or prevent the phenomenon, even though the scientific basis for these strategies is doubtful. As we have seen, the greatest breakthrough in research has been the discovery of the relation between sleeping position and the phenomenon of crib death. We hope that a new wave of studies will continue the process of wiping out this mysterious killer in the near future.

18

"Be patient! He'll grow out of it"

The Stubborn Nature of Sleep Disturbances

A widespread myth, not only among the general public but also among many professionals, is that sleep disturbances in early childhood are necessary developmental pains that disappear by themselves, without a trace, when the child grows up. Parents are advised by professionals and friends, "Wait! Be patient, and the child's sleep problem will solve itself when he grows up a bit." Parents sometimes have a particular unconscious reason for resisting treatment of the sleep problem. These parents readily accept the view that the problem requires no treatment or has no solution. But parents who arrive at the sleep clinic exhausted after coping with the problem for two years or longer are often amazed to learn that the problem can be solved in only a few meetings.

Even though sleep problems do pass or improve with age in many cases, it doesn't always happen. In most cases, in fact, the problem remains but changes its nature. The child continues to awaken and suffer from the problem, but because he doesn't bother his parents anymore, they believe that the problem is solved. Much data point to the chronic nature of these problems. In a comprehensive study

conducted on the subject of early childhood sleep disturbances, it was found that 10 percent of mothers reported
that their babies awakened three or more times each
night. Eight percent of the mothers reported that their
child needs an hour or more to return to sleep after awakening. Five percent reported that their sleep was most
disturbed by the baby. In all, 18 percent of the mothers
reported at least one problem out of the three. At age
three years, 29 percent of these children had problems in
going to bed, falling asleep, or remaining asleep. Out of
all the children who had problems at age eight months,
41 percent still had problems when they were three years
old. Only 26 percent of the children who had sleep problems at age three years had had no problems when they
were examined at eight months of age.

In another study it was found that almost half of the
children who suffered from awakenings at the age of three
years had done so since birth. Forty percent of the children with sleep problems at age eight years had suffered
from them since the age of three years or younger. Yet
another study examined the persistence of sleep problems
over three years among a population of children whose
initial average age was two years. The researchers found
that after three years, the sleep problems remained among
84 percent of the children. The persistence of sleep problems was found to increase along with environmental
stress factors, and to change in inverse proportion to the
mother's educational level. The scientists concluded that
early detection and intervention are important to the child
and the family.

Longitudinal studies that examined the chronic nature of sleep problems also revealed that childhood sleep
problems are an essential cause of adult sleep problems.
It was found that in many cases teenagers and adults who
suffered from sleep problems described having sleep dif-

ficulties since childhood. In another study it was found that children who suffered from problematic sleep-wake rhythm during their first year were more likely to suffer in later years from such problems as difficulty falling asleep, sleep talking, and rhythmic body movements during sleep. Another study examined adults who have difficulty falling asleep and staying asleep. The findings pointed to essential differences in sleep patterns among adults who suffered from sleep problems in childhood and those whose sleep problems began in adulthood. Those who suffered from sleep disturbances in childhood needed a longer time to fall asleep, slept less, and had significant changes in the structure of sleep itself. In other words, chronic sleep problems from childhood were more severe and caused long-ranging changes in the victims' sleep.

The studies show that early childhood sleep disorders do not disappear by themselves among almost half of the children who experience them. Even though the nature of sleep difficulties may change over the course of development, the difficulties themselves continue throughout childhood and into adulthood. Sleep disorders may continue to damage the child's functioning and may become a chronic problem, one that is difficult to treat in adulthood. It is probable that untreated, ongoing sleep difficulties cause structural changes at the physiological level via maturational and developmental processes. When this system stabilizes and loses its plasticity, sleep problems may become even more ingrained and resistant to change and treatment.

19

"To sleep or not to sleep, that is the question!"

Difficulty Falling Asleep and Staying Asleep

hen parents seek treatment for their child's sleep problems, they often need to cope with difficult issues about themselves and their baby. They might wonder, for example, whether something is wrong with the baby, or whether they are failing to fulfill their parental role and thus causing their baby to suffer. These questions become more urgent when parents find themselves unable to solve their child's problem while seeing other parents who have not faced this problem or have solved it easily.

As in any complex system, a sleep problem may stem from various sources. Its consequences and solutions are similarly varied. One way to try to solve a baby's sleep problem is by using medication, specifically sedatives. Most professionals use this approach, which directly influences the nervous system, only for babies with the most extreme sleep disorders because medication has undesirable effects and is often ineffective for common problems in early childhood.

A second approach is behavior therapy, in which specific changes in the parents' behavior are intended to alter the child's sleep patterns. First, the parents are advised how their behavior, and changes in it, can influence the child's behavior. They may also be given guidance about how to understand thought processes, so that they can evaluate their own expectations and feelings about the baby, and comprehend what the sleep problem means to them. Parents can then examine their feelings about their role as parents, their child's significance to them, and what role the sleep problem plays in the parent-child relationship. Ideally, the parents can change their behavior based on what they have learned, and these changes lead to a change in the child's behavior as well. This type of treatment is called psychodynamic therapy, family therapy, or parent-child therapy.

Research and clinical experience from a spectrum of fields in treating babies and children teach us that each intervention in the all-encompassing system that influences the child's behavior also influences other components of the system. In clinical work in the field of sleep disorders, we often combine therapeutic components of different approaches in order to increase the treatment's efficacy and to shorten its duration. The following survey describes the various components of infant sleep-disorder treatment. Because giving medication is problematic and usually not recommended, it will be discussed briefly first, after which different approaches will be described in greater depth.

Medication

Medication for sleep is used widely for children. Studies show that between 25 percent and 50 percent of children received medication for sleep or sedatives at a young age. Clinical experience and the findings of many studies, however, have found little efficacy in medication. Medication for sleep usually has little positive influence on sleep problems at a young age, and what influence it has is typically temporary, disappearing immediately after treatment ends. Many parents hesitate to give their children medication for sleep, with good reason. Ongoing prescription of medications for adults with sleep problems has been shown to have negative effects. Nonetheless, many doctors recommend sedatives, at least in the short term, in an attempt to change the child's sleep habits and in the hope that the change will lead to subsequent improvement. Some doctors see medication as a way to calm exhausted parents, who in nighttime moments of crisis can use sedatives to calm the child and get a few hours of sleep themselves.

Sleep medication should be used as a means of treatment for sleep disorders in young children only in extreme cases that are nonresponsive to behavioral interventions. This conclusion is based, to a great extent, on the high efficiency of behavioral-psychological treatment methods for these problems.

Behavioral Therapy

Donald Winnicott stated in one of his writings that there is no such thing as a baby without a mother. What he meant by this provocative statement was that the baby lives and functions in relation to figures that are significant to him, and that most of his behavior is influenced by and is a response to his parents' behavior, their moods, and their expectations of him. Indeed, many studies point to the close relation between parental personalities and behavioral patterns on the one hand, and their child's sleep disturbances on the other. The studies support the assumption that parents exert great influence on the developing sleep patterns of their child. Methods of behavioral therapy are largely based on work with the parents. The goal of therapy is understanding the possible sources of the problem in coping with the child's sleep problem and consolidating more effective coping strategies. The treatment itself must be based on early evaluation of the type of problem from which the child suffers, in order to ensure that the treatment method is appropriate for it. But traditional behavioral therapy does not deal with analyzing the sources of the parents' problems and with their personality dynamics. These aspects are unique to dynamic therapy or to therapies that combine behavioral and dynamic principles.

Several of the existing behavioral methods in the field will be detailed in the following section. These are ways in which parents can act and react in order to aid their child to cope with difficulties in falling asleep or with frequent or lengthy awakenings during the night. These awakenings are related to a demand for involvement, parental presence, or help. The behavioral methods will be ineffective if the problem stems from medical reasons or if more complex psychological problems in the parent-child relationship exist, requiring further assessment and treatment.

Behavioral therapy is based on the assumption that the source of the child's problems falling asleep and staying asleep is often a need to have her parents nearby in order to self-soothe, because she hasn't learned to fall asleep by herself in her own bed and to spend the night on her own. The basic assumption behind the therapy is that if the parents help the child learn how to calm herself and fall asleep by herself, she won't need them during the night; her sleep will then become continuous and more independent. An additional assumption is that because parental presence and the parent-child relationship are important to the child, she in effect receives a "reward" for her crying and for awakening at night, the reward being closeness to the parents. These rewards encourage the problematic behavior. One of the tasks that the parents must undertake is to teach the child to distinguish between night and day and between the parent-child relationship during the day and the clear expectation of quiet and noninvolvement at night. Behavioral therapy can thus be described as a weaning process. As in weaning from breast-feeding, sometimes the baby is the first to signal that she has lost interest and prefers substitutes, and sometimes the mother initiates the process. And as in the weaning process, too, behavioral therapy for problems falling asleep and staying asleep often leads to temporary distress and a reactive protest by the baby. These reactions make it hard for many parents to accomplish the weaning, and they often need professional help to avoid having the problem dragged on for years.

Based on this logic, most of the methods focus on narrowing or "extinguishing" parental involvement, and in so doing, helping the child develop her own ability to calm down and fall asleep. It is important to note that not all methods are effective to the same degree, and some are hard to put into practice, both for the parents and for the baby.

"Ignore Him"

This method stops cold turkey all bedtime rituals that demand parental involvement. The goal of the method is to teach the child that crying is ineffective and won't lead to parental involvement. The parents must put the child to sleep and must not go to him afterward at all during the night. Even when the child protests and cries at

Are We Being Cruel to the Baby?

One of the questions that bothers many parents about the behavioral therapy methods described in this chapter is whether they are hurting their baby or being cruel to her by not immediately responding to her distress. The best answer to this emotionally loaded question is: No! In many cases, by using this method, parents end a cycle of ongoing suffering, both for them and for the baby. Before treatment, in many cases, the baby becomes a victim of the parents' anger and impatience because of her nocturnal "abuse." Parents may also express their feelings of helplessness toward the baby during the day. But when we examine, both in therapy and in research studies, how the baby responds to the parents' "cruel" strategy of letting her cry, the response is generally positive. Although she may protest for a day or two, if the rules of the treatment are consistently applied, the sleep problem is usually solved. Moreover, most parents report a general improvement in the baby's behavior and mood. Except in unusual cases, no signs of emotional distress are reported.

length, the parents must absolutely ignore it. Any gesture to calm or encourage the child or to intervene in any way undermines the effectiveness of the strategy because each such action may cause the child to expect the parent to become once again the familiar "good" parent. The child may assume that all he has to do is to continue protesting until his parents "break." The baby does not "plan" his actions as an older child would, but he reacts according to simple rules of cause and effect. Totally ignoring the crying baby is a difficult treatment method for many parents to implement; they cannot stand to hear their child cry at length. Many parents fear that they are causing the child trauma and a sense of abandonment. Implementation of this method, with its sudden lengthy detachment, may create a significant emotional problem for the parents, and perhaps for the baby as well. Many babies, despite their exhaustion, are unable to lie down again after a long crying spell, and if the parents cannot enter the room even to help the child resume a sleeping posture, the strategy may actually delay his falling asleep.

Gradual Weaning

The principle that guides the gradual-weaning approach holds that direct conflict and the child's emphatic protest can sometimes be prevented. If the steps to weaning are carried out gradually, then the change will be less difficult for the child. The end goal of the child's self-soothing is achieved in stages. Treating a baby who learned to fall asleep only while being rocked and breast-fed, for example, takes place in stages. In the first stage, the mother finishes breast-feeding while the baby is still awake, under lighted conditions and without moving him about a lot. When the baby finishes feeding, after a break, the mother turns off the light and puts him to sleep in her arms with gentle rocking. In the next stage, after the distinction has been made between feeding and falling asleep, the mother puts the baby in his crib and sits next to him while rocking the baby until he falls asleep. In the third stage, the mother only sits next to the child, without touching or looking at him, and waits until he falls asleep. The next stage calls for the mother to move away from the crib as the baby is falling asleep. And in the final stage, after the previous goals have been achieved, the mother puts the baby into his crib and leaves the room while he is awake, and he puts himself to sleep. At each stage, the child may protest. He may cry, scream, and show other signs of distress. The parent must be able to withstand this behavior and not relent or detour from the behavior that had been decided upon for each stage of the process. The major drawback of this method is that it may become an ongoing nightmare if the child has a difficult reaction to each stage. For these babies, a faster approach is often preferable.

In many cases, the gradual approach is easier for parents who feel that they can prevent a head-on confrontation with the child by avoiding a drastic change in the bedtime routine. Often, even as they are deciding to seek treatment, the parents have begun to initiate small changes to wean the child from nighttime parental presence. Sometimes the baby responds positively to a small step toward change. One couple, for example, reported that after they made an appointment with me at the sleep laboratory, they decided to stop the pattern of letting their one-and-a-half-year-old baby fall asleep in their arms. The mother continued to put the child to bed and to stay next to his crib, holding his hand until he fell asleep. During the first three days, the child indeed insisted that the mother sit next to him until he fell asleep. But afterward she felt that there was no need for this, and the baby no longer insisted on it. The problem of putting him to bed was solved even before they began treatment. All that was left for us to cope with was his nighttime awakenings.

Checking

This approach is based on a combination of principles that make it popular among professionals. According to this approach, after completing the accepted bedtime rituals that are performed away from the baby's crib while he is awake, the parents put him into his crib, say "goodnight," and leave the room. If the child cries or calls out to his parents, they wait a full five minutes and then one of them returns to the room, returns the child to a sleeping position, makes a brief soothing statement, and leaves the room without additional involvement. If the child continues to cry or to call his parents, they again wait five minutes and respond as they did before, briefly visiting the child and returning him to a sleeping position, if necessary. If the child is quietly awake and is not crying strongly or giving distress signals, the parents do not go to him. Rather, they wait and allow him to fall asleep on his own. If the child awakens again during the night, the parents wait five minutes and once again make a brief visit to his room. Parents who adopt this strategy are taught that they cannot prevent the child's awakenings during the night, but they can allow him to learn to calm himself and put himself back to sleep, both at the beginning of the night and during its course. The child meanwhile learns that he has not been "deserted." His parents continue to exist for him, and he can see them at given time intervals. But they also relay the message to him that they will not "help" him fall asleep. The child has intervals in which he can calm himself and fall asleep on his own. The original approach developed by Prof. Richard Ferber is slightly different. According to Ferber's method the time intervals are gradually lengthened, beginning with three minutes, going to five, then ten, and so on.

Clinical and research experience has shown that after an appropriate assessment and guidance, the response to this treatment approach occurs within two to three days if the parents are able to apply it without reservation. The impression from various studies is that parents have an easier time applying this method than more radical approaches, and this is expressed in the child's immediate response.

Positive Rewards

Children a bit older and more verbal (usually three years old and up) can be actively involved in the treatment process. Once the parents understand the emotional difficulties that may be the source of the child's sleep disturbance, a sort of "contract" can be established in which goal behaviors are established and a "reward" promised if the child keeps up her end of the "deal." A child who insists on falling asleep in her parents' bed, for example, or awakens at night and steals into their bed to sleep with them, can be offered an arrangement according to which each time she succeeds in sleeping through the entire night in her own bed, she receives a special decorative "sticker" in the morning, which she puts on a bulletin board. After receiving a certain predetermined number of stickers — signifying that the child has essentially overcome her problem — she receives a more important reward to reflect that success. When we give great importance to the "contract" and enlist the child's motivation (whether to win the reward or to please her parents or a professional who aids in the treatment), this approach has an extremely high chance of success. Often, when the problem is more complex, this approach can help in a therapeutic framework that clarifies additional possible sources of the child's difficulties — for example, anxiety that causes him to fight for sleeping with his parents. The combination of the behavioral approach in therapy of this type lets the child know that even if he has reasons to be fearful or anxious, the parents, who understand his difficulties, also believe that he can overcome the problem.

Sometimes the child lacks sufficient motivation for

positive reinforcement to work, and negative reinforcement — a response calculated to make the existing solution unacceptably unpleasant for the child — should be combined with it. The next case exemplifies this strategy.

Three-year-old Michelle insisted on stealing into her parents' room at night and joining them to sleep. Her sleeping with them wouldn't have bothered her parents if Michelle had slept quietly and let them continue sleeping. But unfortunately, even in their bed, Michelle continued to be restless, insisting that her mother wake up and attend to her until she fell asleep. This was repeated several times over the course of the night. Because of this, the mother was exhausted, and the father moved to Michelle's room to sleep on the sofa whenever Michelle came into their bed.

Michelle developed a rapport with me very quickly. She had very good expressive ability and explained to me that she wanted to be like big people and sleep with Mommy and Daddy. She also told me that she was not interested in solving the problem that bothered her parents because she "loved to sleep with Mommy." Her parents' distress didn't concern her, and it was clear that the child, who was very controlling and knew how to stand her ground during our meetings, would not change her pattern without having a good reason for doing so. The parents reported that they tried to tempt Michelle with all different kinds of treats and offers as incentives to stay in her own bed, but to no avail. At this stage, I decided that there was no choice but to combine two vital components in treatment — in common language, "the stick and the carrot." I checked with the parents to see just how determined they were to solve the problem, and after satisfying myself that they indeed were intent on doing so, I explained to them and to Michelle that they were about to solve the problem immediately.

Michelle looked uninterested, but in fact she was listening carefully to every word. I explained to her parents that beginning that night, Michelle would not come into their room any more. And each night that she didn't come into their room, she would get to choose a special sticker. After she collected ten stickers, she would get a special reward for overcoming the problem. Understandably, Michelle and her parents reacted to this plan in astonishment, and her parents asked what they should do if Michelle came to their room. I suggested that they put her back in her room and warn her that the next time they'd have to lock her door. Like many other parents, Michelle's parents had reservations about this suggestion. I made it clear that closing the door was to be done only after a warning, and that it should be only for a brief time, in order to convey to Michelle their ability to limit her undesirable behavior and their total control over the situation. If she chose to continue sleeping in her own bed, the door would remain open. After the parents understood the principle, they agreed to the approach. Michelle looked very reserved.

At the next meeting, the parents reported immediate success. They said that on the first night, Michelle came to their bed, but after one warning, she remained in her own bed after calling to them and being calmed verbally from afar (as had been agreed upon in advance). During the following days, Michelle proudly collected the stickers and was about to receive a dollhouse, which was the promised reward for overcoming the problem.

Soothing Aids

The baby's ability to self-soothe is an important part of her ability to fall asleep on her own and to maintain continuous sleep. Soothing aids or transitional objects serve as a means of calming down without parental presence, usually for children aged two years and up. Soothing aids are usually objects that the child chooses from her natural environment or that her parents offer her. It is sometimes possible to encourage the process when the parents talk about "the teddy bear getting tired" and wanting to sleep in the child's bed. The child lays the teddy bear in her bed and "calms" him, and the symbolic game reinforces the parents' effort to calm the child. So too, the teddy bear's presence in her bed eases the feeling of loneliness and its accompanying anxieties. This straightforward approach does not involve any difficulties. Still, it is hard to predict whether the child will respond to the approach. Many children refuse to adopt a transitional object of this type, and sometimes the "adoption" doesn't have ramifications on their sleep problem. Prof. Thomas Anders studied, with some success, the possibility of teaching babies from a young age to develop a bond with a transitional object such as a shirt that has the mother's smell, and the question of whether this type of bonding will help these babies' sleep. A sleep watch that we give to babies for follow-up on their sleeping is often referred to as a transitional object. Parents report that the child becomes attached to the watch, reminds them to put it on her, and has trouble separating from it. In certain cases, the parents also see an improvement in the baby's sleep, which they associate with the use of the sleep watch.

Constant Presence

This method is based on the assumption that the child's basic problem is separating from the parents at night. Problems falling asleep or staying asleep manifest his continual attempts to ensure that his parents are in the immediate vicinity. A parent's total presence in the room while the child sleeps can calm him and may allow him to overcome his anxiety over sleep and the separation that is involved in it. This method demands that one of the parents sleep next to the child's bed for one continuous week, from the minute that the child is put to sleep until he wakes up in the morning. The parent sleeping next to the child doesn't respond to the child and doesn't take him out of his bed during the night. He sleeps or pretends to be sleeping, with no eye contact and no verbal contact with the child. The message to the child is that he doesn't need to worry and check for parental presence during the night. The parent is with him all the time but also demonstrates to him that at night we sleep. Parents often try this method partially and are surprised to learn that although the child appears to be asleep, he immediately reacts to their attempts to steal out of the room. This experience may teach the baby that he must be persistent and on guard in order to prevent attempts to abandon him. To avoid conveying such an unintended lesson, the parent must make a real commitment to spend the nights continuously with the child. Many children respond quickly to this message, and the parents discover at the end of the week that the child has calmed down and no longer checks for their presence.

This approach is especially appropriate when the child shows signs of general separation anxiety — clinging to the mother, for example, or reacting badly to her absence during the day. Likewise, it is appropriate in many cases for parents who have parental separation anxiety, which makes it hard for them to apply approaches that focus on rapid weaning.

Scheduled Awakenings

This approach is based on the assumption that over time a close relation is created between the internal clock that dictates the child's awakenings at night and the parents' reaction and treatment of the child. This relation generates a timetable of awakenings, often as precise as a clock. The goal of the scheduled awakenings is to disrupt the activity of the internal clock that led to the spontaneous awakenings and to what came in their wake. In this approach, the parents awaken the child about a half-hour before his spontaneous awakening. This method is hard to apply due to the fact that many parents have trouble knowing when exactly to wake the child or are emotionally opposed to waking a sleeping child as part of treatment.

Psychodynamic Therapy

Treatment principles of dynamic therapy are based on the attempt to understand the wishes, difficulties, attitudes, and fantasies of parents regarding their baby in general, and about the sleep problem specifically. In many cases, this understanding, which helps parents interpret the internal battles involved in these issues, aids them, too, in unleashing stoppers and automatic and stereotypical ways of thinking and acting, and to think and apply different possible ways of relating to and acting with their baby. Sometimes, removing an emotional barrier related to parenting helps the baby to discover and experience his parent in a new way, and this is a quick enough solution to the sleep problem. The following case study exemplifies some principles of dynamic therapy.

For as long as she could remember, Dafna longed for the day she would become a mother. Her strong desire for a child grew with the years, and as a young woman she had relationships with many men, hoping that one would lead to marriage and the desired child. Unfortunately, for reasons that Dafna could not explain, all her relationships ended in disappointment. Concerned by the ticking of her biological clock, when Dafna was thirty-five years old she decided to have a child even without finding a life partner. She convinced one of her casual friends to aid her, assuring him that he would be free from all paternal responsibility. Dafna was very happy and satisfied when she held Dan, after so many years of anticipation and fantasies of motherhood.

Dafna was a career woman who enjoyed great status in a senior position in an office, and she was sure that she could combine her professional career with single-parent mothering, even if it meant having to compromise and give up a little in her career. When Dan was two months old, she found a skilled caretaker who calmed her fears and allowed her to return to work full of confidence that Dan was in good hands. The hours that Dafna was with Dan were full of enjoyment for her. It appeared that her great wish had come true.

Only one thing clouded the happy picture. As Dan grew, he became more demanding, both day and night. He would awaken several times and demand his mother's care: feeding, pampering, and calming. With time, this pattern worsened, and Dafna had to spend long hours with Dan over the course of the night. Even when she broke down and agreed to let him sleep in her bed, he continued to wake up and demand her care at night. Dafna felt that the nighttime problems and her lack of regular sleep turned her world upside down and hurt her ability to function at work. Likewise, Dan's growing demands made it impossible for her to go out at night and develop social relationships for fear that Dan would terrorize a babysitter. Dafna felt that she was becoming antagonistic toward Dan, and as a result she became filled with guilt. In the end, when Dan was two and a half years old and Dafna was on the brink of despair, she turned to the sleep clinic for advice in solving Dan's sleep problem.

During the first meeting, Dafna described the situation up until the current low point. An evaluation of sleep at home showed that Dan's sleep was indeed disrupted. At the second meeting, the therapist related to Dafna's distress with great empathy, based on the difficult picture of Dan's sleeping and Dafna's need to cope with the problem alone. Dafna, who was on the brink of tears, focused on her distress and described her difficult negative feelings about the child. At this point, she burst into bitter tears and calmed down only after a long silence. The therapist concentrated on the difficulty that Dafna felt due to her anger toward her child. Dafna explained, crying continuously, that she had thought that she would never get sick of her child. Later Dafna told about her childhood in the shadow of difficult events that she had experienced. Her father, who had not wanted a child, left home only weeks after she was born. Her mother was continually depressed and was never nurturing. Instead, she needed Dafna to support her. As Dafna described her childhood, her problems in adulthood became more comprehensible. The ramifications of Dafna's lack of a relationship with a father figure emerged in her difficulties in creating stable relationships with men. In her choice to become a single parent, she replayed — unconsciously, of course — the circumstances of her life without a father. Dan's sleep problem turned her into an unsuccessful mother, as her mother had been for her. The drama of her own childhood was created anew, in diametric opposition to all her conscious wishes and desires.

Therapy continued with a focus on Dafna's coping with the clarification of her understanding of the similarity between her difficult childhood and her motherhood with Dan. To help deal with Dafna's guilt feelings, her therapist pointed out her talents and her intact personality and functional state, in stark contrast to her mother's sit-

Can Parents Solve Sleep Problems by Themselves?

In a comprehensive study done in the United States, parents of 235 children aged twelve to thirty-five months, taken from a normal sample representative of the population, were interviewed. The parents were asked about their children's sleep problems, about the ways in which they tried to cope with these problems, and about the degree of success they had with the methods they used.

More than 70 percent of parents reported that they tried different known methods, such as letting the child cry until he calmed down, letting the child cry with "visits" at set intervals, giving him some object to help him calm down, allowing him to sleep with parents, and so on. Of those who tried these methods, approximately 70 percent reported success. It can be concluded, then, that many parents can solve their children's sleep problems by using knowledge they acquired from books, media, or friends. Parents who seek help from experts are those who failed in independent attempts to solve the problems.

One of the interesting data that arose from the study was that 36 percent of the parents reported that they tried using automobile movement as a method to put their baby to sleep. These parents usually stated that they didn't succeed in putting the child to sleep any other way. I was shocked the first time that parents told me that the father took the baby for a car ride of twenty minutes at 4 A.M. in order to put him to sleep. Later I learned from many parents that this pattern is not at all extraordinary.

uation. Dafna gradually felt strengthened and came to believe that she could change her future with Dan. She decided that instead of being frustrated and feeling aggressive toward Dan for "bothering" her at night, she could set limits and stand up to his demands without feeling that she was becoming a bad and frustrating mother. In the process of the rapid and successful change, Dafna did not need concrete or technical advice about dealing with Dan during the night. After the guilt subsided, she could implement solutions that were clear to her; those became the "right" answers, which allowed her to perceive herself as a good parent.

Dafna and Dan's story demonstrates the power that childhood history has in shaping parenting patterns in adulthood. Selma Fraiberg, a psychoanalyst who has contributed greatly to understanding this subject, observed that every parent enters her child's room carrying with her the ghosts from her own childhood. Psychodynamic therapy focuses on understanding the conscious and unconscious variables that form parenting and all of its aspects. Understanding the dynamic sources of parental behavior can, in many cases, lead to a change in perceptions, in parental emotional reactions, and in behavior toward the child, and these changes can help solve the sleep problem. Counseling the parents in specific behavioral methods is not always necessary. In many cases, though, the understanding and manner of relating in psychodynamic therapy can be combined with specific counseling for parents, speeding up the therapeutic process and making it more efficient. Often, behavioral therapies fail because they don't relate to dynamic aspects that motivate parental behavior, in particular their opposition to treatment or the therapist's advice, or their failure to apply the advice given to them.

20

"My child is possessed"

Family and Personal Dynamics of the Parents

A baby who suffers from sleep problems creates a lot of "noise" (with all its implications) in the family system. This noise can be expressed by the parents when they feel frustrated and helpless and that they are unfit parents, or when they blame each other for causing the problem and for their inability to solve it. In these cases, parents who consult a sleep specialist expect a mediator who will rule on the question of what to do and on which one of them has the right approach. When the parents' relationship is problematic for other reasons, the sleep problem adds fuel to the fire. In these cases, treatment of the child's sleep problem is not enough. The couple's problems must be treated as well.

Sometimes treating the sleep problem appears to offer a solution (as problematic as it is) for the couple's own distress and difficulties. In these cases, the child's sleep problem allows the parents to join forces against a common "enemy" and to fight the problem together. In other cases, the child's sleep problem serves as a way of avoiding conflicts in the couple's relationship. Sometimes, for example, a baby or young child may insist upon sleeping with his parents, or only with his mother. The baby's "banishment" of the father from the marriage bed can serve as a "solution" to the parents' problematic sexual relationship; the baby serves as "birth control." In such cases, we must establish whether the parents' solution is truly acceptable to them and evaluate whether to treat the child's sleep problem separately or within the framework of the larger family system with its other problems.

In most instances, the child's sleep problems and the processes involved in solving them go hand in hand with the parents' sensitive and significant issues. These sensitive issues are often at the root of the sleep problems, and they must be dealt with simultaneously. A parent who should be allowing the baby to sleep alone yet considers this abandonment, for example, will have difficulty with this task. He or she will have an even harder time coping with the child's prolonged protests. This kind of parent will have a hard time accepting advice to "keep your distance and free the child from his dependence on you." The treatment process must deal with the personal dynamic underlying the parent's problem.

Clinicians frequently ask whether it is possible to focus on and solve just one specific problem, such as the child's sleep problem, while a major family disruption exists. To examine this issue my colleagues and I conducted a study in which brief and focused treatment for the child's sleep problem was suggested to all of the parents who entered the clinic without predetermining which families were "appropriate" for treatment. The result was that many families who seemed particularly difficult to treat because of a myriad of problems, or because of the parents' personalities or psychopathology, were significantly helped by a short-term treatment focused on their child's sleep problem.

One of the surprises in this study may be illustrated

by the story of Rachel, a thirteen-month-old baby whose parents turned to me because of her long-term problem of awakening at night. Rachel's night wakings made her family's life unbearable. Her low-income parents lost patience with her and couldn't endure much more. They developed harsh, negative images, thoughts, and wishes about her. My first impression of the parents was severe. They appeared to have limited emotional resources, displayed limited intellectual ability, and during the discussion were observably helpless and dependent. Because of my evaluation of them, I doubted whether what I offered would help them. During the meeting that took place after the initial evaluation, the parents continued to tell more and more about how tired and helpless they were, and seemed barely able to listen to what I had to say. I offered the "checking approach" to these parents, a technique that allows the parent to check on the child during the night only at scheduled times. Toward the end of the meeting, the father asked me: "Will you be able to see, according to what's recorded on the sleep watch, if we really went in to her every five minutes?" This question exemplified his concrete manner of thinking.

Rachel's parents left me with the clear feeling that this case was doomed from the outset. To my surprise, when they returned after a week of implementing the program according to my instructions, they reported significant success. These parents had stubbornly stuck to the plan, had endured the emotional anguish that they felt along the way, and had achieved significant positive results. They reported a serious easing of the child's sleep problem and were profuse in their thanks. At the follow-up session six months later, the treatment goals had been maintained. This case and others like it show that the existence of pervasive problems in parental functioning and other parental limitations does not preclude the parents' being able to grasp the concrete-technical aspects of an intervention, to implement it, and to resolve the specific problem.

Another family dynamic that has appeared in several cases can create major difficulties with treatment. Guy was a ten-month-old boy who was referred with a problem of prolonged awakening throughout the night. When he woke he insisted on his mother's presence, care, feeding, and lengthy holding. After the initial consultation and attempt at implementing my advice, the mother claimed that no change had occurred and that she didn't believe that the family could be helped. Conversely, the father claimed that there was a significant improvement at first. After a few good nights came a bad night, however, the mother assumed that the child was sick and regressed to her old behaviors. The contradiction in the parental reports suggested that the mother had her own seemingly paradoxical reasons for prolonging the problem. Additional investigation revealed that Guy had a brother older by three and a half years who was fiercely jealous of him. Each time the mother went to take care of Guy during the day, the brother had a temper tantrum, cried, broke things, and banged his head against the wall with frightening force. The parents reported feeling helpless in coping with this jealousy, and the only "solution" they had found was minimizing the amount of care the mother gave Guy during the day, while his brother was around. As a result, Guy spent most of his day in a playpen and received little care or physical contact with his mother. It became clear that the "stolen" time at night was the only way that Guy and his mother found to fulfill some of their natural needs for closeness and affection. The mother was able to set clear limits at night only after she learned to cope with the other child's jealousy during the day. She was then able to get close to Guy during the day. Guy's sleep problem was quickly resolved.

Guilt is another significant issue that comes up during treatment of early-childhood sleep disorders. Parents often feel guilty because they believe that their child's sleep problem proves that something is physically wrong with the child and that they are the cause of this "defect."

Gad was fourteen months old when he was referred to me because of numerous and lengthy awakenings at night. During the initial evaluation the mother immediately brought up her fear that her son's sleep problems were caused by some sort of organic problem. Through heart-rending tears she added that she thought that Gad had this problem because she had been depressed for a long time during her pregnancy. She had felt, as soon as he was born, that something was wrong with him. The mother's revelation of this experience during the consultation was significant. Even more significant was the fact that this was the first time she had discussed the subject with her husband. After the consultation, the parents carried out a weeklong follow-up, after which they reported that they had never had such a good week since Gad was born. The mother apologized for having "wasted my time," because no sleep problem was actually detected. I pointed out the possibility of spontaneous change, especially in light of the mother's having gone through a significant experience that eased her burden, an experience that may also have been absorbed by her son in some way. The parents did an additional week's successful follow-up, and the sessions ended. At a follow-up meeting a few months later, they reported that the sleep problem had not recurred. Apparently, the mother's ability to have a warm emotional relationship with her son had been disrupted as a result of the guilt she had experienced during her pregnancy, perhaps because of unconscious anger, and from the feeling that she had been "punished" by getting a "damaged" baby. The relief from her guilt feelings changed something in the way she experienced her child, and this apparently brought about the significant improvement in his sleep patterns.

Parental guilt and helplessness may also increase during treatment, when parents see the prospect of quickly solving the sleep problem as proof of their failure as parents and as proof of their role in creating the problem. These feelings can create an unconscious need to resist treatment to avoid having these feelings of guilt and failure validated. In these cases, the parents can be helped to accept the child's sleep problem with understanding. They can see it as arising from, among other things, his vulnerability and his unique needs, and from their understandable difficulty finding a way to meet his special needs.

The personality dynamics of the parents can sometimes be an impassable roadblock for short-term therapy. Ron's parents sought treatment because of their twenty-month-old son's prolonged night wakings. At bedtime and during his nocturnal awakenings, Ron was demanding and made his parents go through varied and complex ceremonies. He wanted them to calm him, for example, by holding him while feeding and rocking him. They then had to continue rocking him at great length in a baby carriage until he fell asleep. He often began his day in the middle of the night and demanded, yet again, the same complicated ceremonies in order to fall asleep. In the course of discussion, I discovered that the parents had recently moved from a kibbutz to the city. One of the major reasons that they had left was their failure to come to terms with the separate sleeping arrangement for children, away from the family home. For a long time Ron slept at home, against the accepted norms of the kibbutz, because of his "sleep problem."

During the first meeting the parents described their

child as someone who totally controlled their lives and bossed them around both day and night. They appeared unable to set any limits. Ron's behavior during the meeting matched their description. He signaled and his parents obeyed. When he decided that he wanted to sit in his mother's chair, she got up and gave him her seat with no protest. When he tried to touch "off-limits" objects in the room, his parents were unable to directly prohibit him. Instead, they tried to beg him or to distract him in a variety of ways. They avoided any assertive interaction with Ron and were unable to establish their authority.

At the next session, the issue of control was broached with the parents. They were counseled about ways of allowing Ron to develop the ability to calm himself and fall asleep by himself, using the checking approach. During this session an emphasis was placed on setting limits for Ron. The parents seemed to accept and understand the importance of what I said and its significance beyond the subject of Ron's sleep problem. They agreed to begin applying the intervention during the upcoming week. A week later the father, who was a large man physically and emanated great power and strength, reported that they were unsuccessful in even beginning to apply what we had agreed upon. He said that whenever he attempted to put Ron into bed, the child protested and resisted physically, and the father did not know what to do. The father feared that if he put Ron to bed in a firmer manner he might "break his bones or his back." This statement clarified the father's enormous difficulty using his power, which he experienced as aggressive and destructive. These feelings were apparently related to deeper layers in his personality structure. I discussed these issues with the parents, and they were encouraged to continue working on establishing limits. Instead, they decided to give up and discontinued the sessions.

Parental limit setting is an important developmental topic that comes up quite often in therapy and is closely tied to the parents' ability to cope with their child's sleep problem. Developmental research shows that children whose parents have trouble setting limits and using their parental authority develop, on the one hand, a distorted feeling of power over their environment; on the other hand, they develop overwhelming anxieties and fears because there is nothing strong that can protect them from external threats and internal drives. In many cases, successful treatment of the child's sleep problem validates the parents' "declaration" to their child that they are in charge. Children accept this message in a more positive way than the parents expect. In many cases, this communication leads to the child's general calming in areas not directly related to the sleep problem.

Just as sleep disorders can arise from problematic family dynamics and become an expression of them, they can also create or complicate problems in the family system. In these cases, the child's sleep problem has complex ramifications for his functioning and the family's functioning. Solving the sleep problem may lead to significant relief in the child's and the family's situation. Dan, twenty months old, developed a significant sleep problem that intensified and was related to severe separation anxiety. The child had trouble sleeping at night, and during the day he absolutely refused to sleep in day care. His caretaker there had a great deal of difficulty coping with the problem and told Dan's parents, on short notice, that they had to take him out of day care. The parents came to me frightened and helpless, with a problem that had grown to unexpected proportions. They had found another day-care center for Dan but feared that the sleep problem would worsen in the new situation and create additional problems. From the evaluation, the child's separation anxiety appeared to have affected many situations before the parents sought therapy. Following the evaluation, a co-sleeping approach was recommended, with one parent sleeping in the child's room for a week. The parents returned a week later significantly relieved. The child had calmed down dramatically, sleeping quietly at night. His separation anxiety and exaggerated clinging to his mother during the day had totally disappeared. The parents still feared that the transition to the new day-care center would reverse the positive change, but no such reversal occurred. Dan adapted relatively well to his new surroundings. His sleep problem had created a complex system of pressures, and its solution created dramatic changes that touched many aspects beyond the sleep problem itself.

Our brief interventions for infant sleep problems are not tailored to explore and unravel complex family dynamics in the way other forms of treatment, such as family therapy or individual psychotherapy, do. However, it is striking how often the discussion of infant sleep triggers these ubiquitous issues of separation, loss, abandonment, spousal relationships, and power struggles. Although in brief interventions we limit our discussion of these issues, it seems that for the parents the opportunity to address them often supersedes the specific sleep problem. As one mother explained, with tears of both pain and relief, "I came to talk to you about why I cannot help my child sleep through the night, and I ended up bringing in my mother to discuss the devastating loss of my father when I was a baby."

21

"Does it really help?"

Research on the Efficacy of Treatment and Its Ramifications

When I started work in the treatment of infant sleep problems I realized that it was one of the most rewarding areas for a clinical child psychologist. The combination of the family's extreme initial distress, the briefness of the intervention, the high success rates of treatment, and the resultant relief for the parents give the practitioner the best possible experience, one that could hardly be matched in any other areas of psychotherapy.

The rapid, successful interventions also challenge common beliefs, such as the injunction to "let the child grow out of the problem." In light of the persistence of sleeping problems and the ongoing price the child and her family pay while they last, it is hard to justify ignoring the available effective interventions.

The effect of clinical interventions with parents of infants who suffer from sleep problems has been studied extensively. Many studies showed that the methods of behavioral treatment described in the previous chapters were effective in quickly solving many babies' sleep problems. These studies were based on parents' reports, and pointed to an improvement in the child's sleeping, even though what precisely changed cannot be concluded from them. Do children's sleep patterns really change in such a brief period of time? Do infants stop waking up, or do they only learn that crying and calling their parents is pointless? In order to clarify these questions, I conducted a comprehensive study at the Technion Sleep Laboratory, in collaboration with Prof. Peretz Lavie. The study concerned the treatment process of fifty babies, aged nine to twenty-four months, who had a sleep problem involving frequent awakenings. In the study we examined the babies' sleep using sleep watches and parental reports for one week before the treatment. We continued to document their sleep throughout the treatment. We used two treatment methods described earlier: the checking approach and constant presence. The children were randomly divided into treatment groups. The parents received guidance for each type of approach, and the treatment process lasted an average of three to four weeks.

The study demonstrated significant success in both treatment methods for most of the babies. Sixty-eight percent of the parents reported a total solution of their baby's sleep problem, and an additional twenty percent reported a significant improvement. In total, nearly ninety percent of the parents indicated that the treatment was a success, and objective measures of the babies' sleep indeed pointed to a substantial improvement. Similar findings are reported in most studies done in the field with different treatment methods. In our study, the two treatment methods were found to be equally efficient. Additional findings of the study taught us that the main dramatic change in children's sleep patterns occurred during the first two days of treatment. During the course of treatment, two major change processes took place: (1) the babies learned to sleep more continuously and to awaken less; and (2) the babies stopped crying and calling out for their parents when they did awaken at night, so that the parents were unaware that some of the babies continued to wake up.

It is important to note that the effectiveness of intervention has been established by dozens of studies. These studies cover diverse intervention methods, including therapy provided by professionals and "self-help" plans guided by books, magazines, and other sources of parenting information. Many parents are capable of applying the knowledge and principles described in these books and magazines with high success rates and without involving professionals. In addition, research has shown that training parents before the child is born can prevent the later development of sleep problems in the child. All this consistent, reliable scientific information indicates that parents should not allow a sleep problem to persist without attempting the diverse optional avenues for change. The established effectiveness of many of these interventions provides parents with a choice of approaches for helping their own baby and enables them to pick the one that best fits their unique family circumstances, parenting style, and other personal preferences.

22

"It's hard to believe that this is the same child"

Changes in the Wake of Treating Sleep Problems

Sometimes during the initial interview, parents describe their great distress stemming from their baby's sleep problem. I then ask what would happen if the child slept through the night without any disturbances. Some parents doubt that my question is serious, others assert that the problem cannot be solved, still others smile broadly and declare that their lives would change dramatically were the problem indeed to be solved. The parents' answer to this seemingly offhand question teaches us that in many cases, parents see the baby's sleep problem as the primary or only source of distress in their lives. At the end of treatment, however, when the parents are so grateful that they cannot find words to express their relief, they often mention other bothersome problems involving the baby, their other children, or themselves.

This reaction at treatment's end highlights several important points. First, of course, regardless of the parents' pretreatment perception, the sleep problem is not the only problem in their lives. Second, the parents have developed trust in their therapist, so they feel comfortable describing another problem. Third, the same parents who so despaired of their ability to solve the sleep problem now display optimism about their ability to focus on an additional problem and solve it. The therapist enters a family system as a catalyst, encouraging the process of change. He must examine whether there really is a need to continue advising the parents or whether they have acquired new tools and need no more concrete advice from the therapist. Often, parents who received help end the treatment process with a great sense of satisfaction, but also with a willingness to seek advice at a later stage of their child's development, when new types of problems arise.

The first, most noticeable, and most significant change that takes place in the course of treating the baby's sleep problem is seen in the parents. The parents have discovered new possibilities for examining and understanding their child and his problems. They have dealt with their emotional difficulties and with their inner struggles related to caring for a baby. They have learned to examine new alternatives in a dialogue with the baby without letting their sensibilities and manner of response be controlled by their fears or strict ideology on the one hand, or by the baby's needs and demands on the other.

Many parents discover their ability to undertake the behavioral-emotional strategies necessary to solve their problems related to child rearing. In many cases, the central question with which they have learned to deal is one of setting limits in their relationship with the child, comprising the dilemmas of dependence versus independence, needs versus exaggerated demands, and the need to be calmed versus the ability to self-soothe. Parents also learn how to carry out a dialogue between themselves to solve a problem in an area that is often laden with emotion and contentiousness. It is therefore not surprising that research in this area shows that successful treatment of babies' sleep problems encourages feelings of heightened parental competence. The parents feel that they are better able to understand their child's behavior, his distress, and his needs. They believe that they can meet his needs by employing parental common sense rather than surrendering to the child's coercion or control. This experience is related not only to the subject of sleep but to other areas of child rearing as well.

The treatment of sleep problems in babies is an area in which the therapist is greatly rewarded. It is difficult to think of many areas in which the therapeutic response is so quick and so positive. In many cases, therapy ends before it has really begun. Making an appointment with a therapist leads to a change and some sort of relief in the parents' emotional attitude to the subject, and the baby responds immediately by changing his sleep patterns. Treatment often ends after the first meeting, during which the parents only describe their problem and have not yet received advice or guidance. Merely meeting with a professional who listens and is a potential source of support often provides emotional relief for the parents, which is immediately translated into a relief in the baby's sleep patterns. The success of different and varied methods of treatment for sleep problems among babies, and the significant improvement in most cases that are treated, hint that a common ground exists in all of these approaches. And this is the change in the way the parents relate to the problem and their emotional standpoint, rather than a particular change they make in their behavior. It is sometimes difficult to understand the character of this change in cases of quick and efficient intervention like that for sleep problems in infancy. It emphasizes, however, the direct link between the baby's functioning and behavior and the parents' emotional status and ways of relating to him.

23

"How can I make sure my new baby won't develop sleep problems?"

Principles of Preventive Treatment

Based on existing research knowledge, we can determine that not only can babies' sleep problems be treated, but some can be prevented. In Amy Wolfson's study, for example, a group of women received guidance during their pregnancies about how to help their child develop healthy sleep habits. A different group of pregnant women received similar attention but no special information on babies' sleep habits. The babies of mothers who had received the guidance were much less likely to suffer from sleep problems than were the babies of mothers who did not receive guidance on the subject. Another study in which parents were trained when their babies were three months old showed that those babies were less likely to have sleep problems at age nine months than babies of parents who did not receive training. These studies demonstrate the efficacy of preventive intervention in the area of child development. Intervention such as this is usually much more effective than treating a problem after it has been developed and established.

The important principles in developing a baby's

normal sleep habits can of course be worded only generally. Parents who know themselves and their abilities, and
who know the infant and her unique needs, should custom-
ize the principles to their own situation. Many children will
develop healthy sleep patterns regardless of their parents'
behavior and even if the parents make every mistake in the
book. Still, the following principles increase the chance
that the baby will acquire good sleep habits:

■ It is essential to clearly distinguish and convey
to the baby from her first days that we sleep at night
and are awake in the daytime. This can be emphasized by keeping her room dark and quiet at night,
and by refraining from moving the child and involving her in social activity at inappropriate hours.

■ Parents should create a ritual or permanent pattern of behavior before bedtime. This can include
bathing, feeding, a story or music and other calming
behaviors or ideas about "quality time."

■ All social rituals, pampering, and feeding should
be terminated before the baby is put into her crib
to go to sleep. The baby should learn to fall asleep
in her crib from a wakeful state even if it involves
a brief protest.

■ Parents should learn to identify their baby's signs
and rhythms of tiredness and to respond appropriately. Changes in the timing of sleep or other considerations can be made gradually and at a very
slow pace, and not in drastic and short interventions.

■ Parents should refrain from exaggerated and
quick reactions to light crying or other forms of protest during the baby's falling asleep process. In
many cases, the baby will soon fall asleep by herself
without trouble or parental intervention.

■ If you enjoy communal sleeping with the baby when she's young, do it happily and out of free choice. If this pattern is adopted as a response to the baby's sleep problems, it may develop into a rigid pattern that will be hard to change later.

■ It is very desirable to refrain from giving the baby sweet food and drink during the night. Parents need not wake their babies for feedings if the babies are healthy and developing well. Their sense of hunger will self-regulate their schedule.

■ The baby's daytime naps do not usually influence her nighttime sleep unless they take place late in the evening. Parents should therefore not try to prevent their occurrence. In most cases, inappropriate prevention of naps leads to more severe problems at night.

■ From the earliest age the child needs significant connection to both her parents. The baby to whom one or both parents are unavailable during the day often develops a pattern of nighttime connection to the missing parent or parents. The parents should devote time to quality time with the child before bedtime, even if it involves coping with sibling rivalry, and even if it is complicated by the parents' work demands and schedules.

■ The child-father bond is essential to the child. In spite of positive tendencies toward paternal involvement in child rearing, many fathers still feel superfluous or are less interested than the mother. Clinical experience shows that paternal involvement greatly helps in preventing the child's sleep problems and in solving them.

Parents should consider these principles as general guidelines and adapt them to the specific circumstances of their own infant and family. They should take into account such issues as the infant's health and family traditions before applying principles with which they are uncomfortable. Many infants will sleep perfectly well regardless of whether their parents adhere to these guidelines, and some will present difficulties even if their parents follow the guidelines assiduously. Nonetheless, there are good reasons to believe that the majority of healthy infants would benefit from the application of these principles.

24

"Sometimes even a good parent feels like throwing the baby out with the bathwater!"

Parting Words of Encouragement to Parents

P arents often feel responsible for all the baby's problems. In their frustration with the baby's nighttime behavior, they may feel guilty about all their feelings of distress, helplessness, and even anger and hate. Here I am assisted again by D. W. Winnicott's theory of the role of maternal feelings of anger and hate toward her baby. Winnicott addressed the common social convention that the mother, who so anticipated the arrival of her baby and readily programmed her entire existence toward raising him, must feel only positive feelings toward him. (Freud also described idealized maternal love this way.) Winnicott held, however, that a mother also has significant negative feelings toward her baby, who may have hurt her body and distorted her appearance during and after her pregnancy, then robbed her of her independence with his dependence on her. Winnicott described how this anger is released by the often harsh and violent sentiments expressed in certain lullabies to the baby (see sidebar).

Over the years, through my personal familiarity with the subject in working with countless parents

A Popular Lullaby

Rock-a-bye, baby,
In the treetop,
When the wind blows
The cradle will rock;
When the bough breaks
The cradle will fall,
And down will come baby,
Cradle and all.

who have coped with sleep resistant babies, I often find myself amazed by the emotional strength that allows parents to continue functioning in spite of their child's sleep problems. Here and there parents use harsh expressions to "let off steam." Not a few parents have made such remarks as "Sometimes I feel like taking the pillow and smothering him when I feel he's doing this to me on purpose." These expressions reflect tremendous distress that is often accompanied by strong guilt feelings. It is important that parents understand that these expressions of distress and anger are natural and need not be the source of guilt. Instead, parents must be able to use their negative emotions as an impetus to searching for a solution to the problem that underlies their distress and may also harm their relationship with the child. I hope that this book has conveyed the message to parents who struggle that they are not alone, and that they too can solve the problem by themselves or with the help of professionals.

25

"Good morning, sun's up, new day!"

The End of the Night Train

The night train of understanding the baby's night life has arrived at its last stop. A gifted baby might have summed up his notes of the journey in the following manner:

"Mommy, Daddy, let me sleep quietly at night. At night, when it seems to you that I'm asleep, I'm actually doing many things. When you think I'm sleeping deeply and quietly, I'm actually becoming refreshed, and my body is growing, too, so that the nurse who measures and weighs me next time will give me a good grade. My brain works hard to remember all the nonsense that you tried to teach me during the day. I know that there were surely important things that you wanted me to remember, but during the day I didn't have enough time to learn all the material from all the books and programs for gifted children that you bombarded me with. The smile you see on my face when I sleep is not because I remembered your attempt at a very funny joke, Daddy. I'm actually exercising my face nerves and muscles so that I'll know how to laugh when you really have a good joke.

"The fact that I don't always want to go to sleep

doesn't mean that I'm not tired. If Daddy would come home earlier from work and we would have some time to spend together, then I'd happily go to sleep. But I don't want Daddy to go to sleep sad without getting a few hugs from me. When I wake up in the middle of the night, it's usually because I'm worried about Mommy, because I haven't seen her for such a long time. Sometimes I also feel like having another bottle of chocolate milk — and that doesn't turn me into an addict! I know that at my age I shouldn't drive Mommy and Daddy crazy in the middle of the night, but if they don't complain about it, then great! I'm spending some more time with them.

"I know that Mommy sometimes complains in the morning that she doesn't have any more strength for me, and that if this goes on she'll break. I also know that Daddy sometimes says that he doesn't understand why they can never take a babysitter and go out to a movie without worrying what type of havoc I'll wreak. I hate it most when they fight. Then Daddy yells that it's about time that I learn how to sleep and stop being a dictator in this house. Mommy answers him that she doesn't understand what he's complaining about, since he never hears anything at night and doesn't get up at all when I cry. It's really not pleasant for me to hear them complaining all day long. Yesterday Daddy said that he heard that there's a sleep laboratory that treats babies' and children's sleep problems, and maybe it's about time that they do something about it. Mommy agreed, and they called and made an appointment. I don't know. It sounds suspicious to me. They might teach Mommy and Daddy some new tricks that I wouldn't like. I'll outsmart them. Tonight I'm going to sleep like an angel and that's that!"

Appendix 1
Methods of Measurement and the Study of Sleep

I n order to obtain the most physiologic data on what occurs during sleep, research has been based on laboratory recordings that require connecting electrodes to the baby. This makes it possible to record brain waves (EEG), muscle activity (EMG), eye movements (EOG), and patterns of breathing and oxygen level in the blood. Detailed information on the stages of sleep and wakefulness during the night, stages of dream sleep, awakenings, breathing patterns and the other characteristics of the child's sleep are derived from the data received from these various channels.

In this type of examination, the child arrives at the sleep laboratory in the evening, the electrodes are connected to various locations, mainly on his head, and he goes to sleep in an insulated room. Young children usually sleep with one of their parents in the room in order to ease the tension and anxiety that can be created by the unique circumstances of the examination. Often, when the child resists the placement of electrodes, they are connected only after he falls asleep. The nighttime examination goes well for many babies, though in some cases the baby's reaction is problematic and the quality of the examination, like the quality of the child's sleep, is undermined.

The continuation of laboratory sleep research has provided a more detailed distinction between the stages of sleep. In addition to dream (REM) sleep, four other stages were identified at different depths of sleep. They were determined according to different physiologic measures. The depth of sleep is expressed by how difficult it is to awaken a sleeping child and is related to sleep's contribution to refreshment and the feeling of alertness after awakening (see sidebar).

The advantage of the laboratory examination is the detailed information that it gives about sleep. Nonetheless, this examination has a few basic problems. First, because of its high cost and other difficulties, it is usually conducted over the course of only one or two nights. Such a short test may give an inaccurate picture of the subject's sleep patterns, particularly in children whose sleep changes from night to night. And because the examination is conducted in conditions that are new and unfamiliar to the child, his or her sleep patterns may be disrupted by the exam itself. Babies sleep different hours over the course of a twenty-four-hour period, and the examination is usually limited to nighttime hours only. An additional limitation of the examination is the lack of comfort that many parents feel about it. This reaction may deter some parents from authorizing the examination. In spite of all these limitations, a laboratory examination is required when there is a need for a full medical assessment of sleep disturbances on a physiologic basis. In recent years, portable equipment has been developed that allows the full examination to be conducted in the child's home.

Direct Observations of the Sleeping Baby

Some of the researchers who began the job of documenting the stages of sleep and wakefulness of babies saw

The Stages of Sleep and Wakefulness
According to EEG Recordings

Calm wakefulness The child is awake and responds. Brain waves are characterized by brain waves at a frequency of 8–12 Hertz (cycles per minute). If we ask the child how he is, he will respond and will report being awake.

Stage 1 "The gate of sleep," or the transition stage to sleep. The brain waves are smaller in amplitude and their frequency is slower (ranges between 2 to 7 Hertz). Muscle tone decreases, and slow, circular eye movements may be seen. Thought is associative and less controlled. The child's responsivity decreases, and the chance of his reporting that he slept resembles the chance that he would report that he was awake, if asked. This ambiguity invokes a professional controversy whether or not to call this stage sleep or wakefulness.

Stage 2 True sleep. In this stage, special phenomena, called sleep spindles and complex K appear in the brain waves. These represent the onset of sleep. A sleep spindle is expressed as a momentary acceleration of the frequency of brain waves (to 12–14 Hertz). The complex K is expressed as a sudden, very short wave that is characterized by a sharp increase in the height of the wave, accompanied by a prominent decrease. The appearance of sleep spindles and complex K events indicate that the subject is sleeping, but this sleep is still superficial and the subject is quite easily awakened from it.

Stages 3 and 4 Deep sleep. These are the stages of deep sleep that are characterized by deep Delta waves (waves at a low frequency of 1–2 Hertz). In stage 3 Delta waves exist 20–50 percent of the time, while in stage 4 Delta waves must be at least 40 percent of activity. It is harder to awaken the child in these stages and some studies show that children do not respond in them except to powerfully strong noise.

Dream sleep (REM) Dream sleep is characterized by rapid eye movements. These movements are clear to see and are different from the slow eye movements of stage 1. No significant eye movements are observed in the other stages. In addition, a significant decrease in muscle tone occurs, which leads to a sort of temporary paralysis of many of the body's muscles.

themselves as researchers not of sleep but of babies' behavior in general. Researchers such as Heinz Prechtl and Peter Wolff have documented behavioral situations of the young baby on the basis of thousands of hours of observation, coding, and analysis. Evelyn Thoman, one of the most creative and prolific researchers of babies' sleep, continues to base her studies on direct observation.

Methods for Home Recording

Unsatisfied with direct observation, other researchers have sought more economical methods for learning about the baby's sleep patterns. One of the most impressive and classic studies in this area is that of Nathaniel Kleitman and Theodore Engelman (1953), which documented the sleep and wake patterns of nineteen babies from birth until the age of six months. Rather than rely on direct observations, the researchers attached instrumentation to the crib in order to document the babies' movements. This instrument records movements of the crib that reflect the babies' activity patterns. This appears to have been the first use of such technique for the study of babies' sleep.

Pressure-Sensitive Mattress

A later method for the documentation of babies' sleep patterns is based on the use of a mattress or sheet that is sensitive to pressure. The device translates the pressure and the changes in pressure applied to the mattress at different points, recording the movements of the baby's limbs, head, chest, and stomach. This recording allows the study of the baby's patterns of activity and rest as well as his breathing patterns.

Video Recording

Thomas Anders contributed a method of time-lapse video recording to study babies' and young children's sleep. In this procedure, a camera is placed in the baby's room, near the crib. The camera is focused on the crib and can function under infrared light, which does not interfere with the perception of darkness. The camera films a sample every few seconds, rather than continuously filming at a faster pace. In this method, a sixty-minute tape can be used to record samples over the course of an entire night. When the tape is played back, the night's events appear as a speeded movie. The recording makes it possible to distinguish among different states of the child's wakefulness and sleep, and it reveals any intervention by the parents. One limitation of video recording is that when the child is in certain postures, it is difficult to identify different body parts, and it thus is hard to distinguish among the various stages of sleep. In addition, the child often "hikes" in his crib and may get out of the effective range of the camera. In spite of the method's limitations, its reliability is considered comparable to full laboratory examinations. It must be noted that although the method is considered to be relatively unobtrusive for babies and their parents, because the baby sleeps in his natural environment and is not connected to any equipment, some parents resist the invasion of privacy that results when a camera penetrates their domestic intimacy and documents what happens in the baby's bedroom.

The methods based on instruments that document the baby's sleep in her crib demand installation of complex equipment in the child's house and are limited to recording only when baby is in her crib. Modern technological advances have aided in overcoming these obstacles and have provided easier access to the study of sleep.

Actigraphy

One of the most advanced methods developed for the study of babies' patterns of sleep and wakefulness is based on a small gauge of activity, the size of a wristwatch, called an actigraph or a sleep watch. The developments of recent years have made recording equipment small and portable and almost imperceptible. The sleep watch is worn on the child's foot or on the wrist. It continuously measures the child's body movements for a week or more at a time. Because patterns of sleep and wakefulness are directly related to body movements, these devices were used in the study of patterns of sleep and wakefulness in field studies — at first, those related to the military, and later also in civilian studies. In my initial work with Prof. Peretz Lavie, Dr. Orna Tzischinsky, and Rachel Epstein at the sleep laboratory of the Technion in Israel, and later with Professors Mary Carskadon, Christian Acebo, and Thomas Anders at the sleep laboratory of the Bradley Hospital in Providence, we have established the use of these instruments for the study of babies and children. The sleep watch provides a detailed picture of the baby's night life, identifying the schedule of falling asleep and awakening and providing information about the quality of sleep. Usually, the parents are asked to complete a sleep diary during the monitoring period. From the knowledge attained from the sleep watch and from the parents' reports, we can learn whether the baby awakens and finds himself alone, calming himself back to sleep, or whether he spends much time quietly awake. Does he call his parents and what do they do to calm him? This information is important in the processes of evaluation and treatment of sleep disturbances of babies, and in order to study the natural developmental process of phenomena related to the baby's sleep.

Sleep Diary

Name: _____ Date (evening): _____

Evening questionnaire (to be completed in the evening when going to sleep)

Exact time of lights out: _____ time it took to fall asleep: _____

Putting to bed done by: 1. Mother 2. Father 3. Other (who?): _____

Were both parents home when the child was put to sleep? 1. Yes 2. No

To what extent are there problems putting to sleep?

      1. None 2. Some 3. Many

To what extent does the child appear to be tired at bedtime?

      1. Not at all 2. Somewhat 3. Very

Mood at bedtime: 1. Terrible 2. Moderate 3. Good

Did s/he sleep during the day? Yes/No

      From _____ (time) till _____ (time)

      From _____ (time) till _____ (time)

Compared to other days, was this a:

      1. Low-activity day

      2. Typical activity day

      3. Very active day

Did any special event take place today (family, social, etc.)? If yes, specify:

Morning questionnaire (to be completed immediately after awakening)

Exact time of morning awakening: _____

How did s/he awaken this morning:

1. By self 2. Parental initiative 3. Other (specify):

Did s/he awaken during the night: Yes/No. If yes, how many times: _____

1. From _____ (time) for _____ (how long);
Intervention: _____

2. From _____ (time) for _____ (how long);
Intervention: _____

3. From _____ (time) for _____ (how long);
Intervention: _____

4. From _____ (time) for _____ (how long);
Intervention: _____

5. From _____ (time) for _____ (how long);
Intervention: _____

6. From _____ (time) for _____ (how long);
Intervention: _____

To what degree is s/he alert this morning?

      1. Not at all 2. Somewhat 3. Very

Morning mood: 1. Bad 2. Moderate 3. Good

Additional comments about the child's sleep:

Parental Reports

Parents constitute the most important source of information about the baby's sleep and wake patterns. Studies show that parents are able to report accurately the schedule of sleep (when the child goes to sleep and when he awakens). Their knowledge of the child's sleep quality, however, is limited. Usually, the most precise way to derive reliable information from the parents is with the help of a sleep diary, which they complete every day (see sidebar). The main problem with sleep diaries is that parents tire of writing in them day after day (or night after night). According to research, within a brief period (one to two weeks), parents become less inclined to keep the diary and report fewer and fewer events related to the child's sleep.

Another method for assessing sleep is based on questionnaires addressing various sleep-related topics. These questionnaires are usually more general and less accurate than a sleep diary.

Appendix 2

A Sampling of Popular Books on Sleep and Nighttime Fears for Very Young Children

Asch, Frank. *Good Night, Baby Bear*. New York: Harcourt, Brace, 1998.

Bauer, Marion Dane, with Jo Ellen McAllister Stammen, ill. *Sleep, Little One, Sleep*. New York: Simon and Schuster, 1999.

Bourgeois, Paulette, with Brenda Clark, ill. *Franklin's Blanket* (Franklin Series). New York: Scholastic Trade, 1995.

Boynton, Sandra. *The Going to Bed Book*, ed. Kate Klimo. New York: Little Simon, 1982.

Brown, Margaret Wise, with Ashley Wolff, ill. *Little Donkey Close Your Eyes*. New York: HarperTrophy, 1999.

Brown, Margaret Wise, with Clement Hurd, ill. *Goodnight Moon*. New York: HarperCollins Juvenile, 1999.

Cazet, Denys. *I'm Not Sleepy*. New York: Orchard, 1992.

Cooper, Helen. *The Boy Who Wouldn't Go to Bed: Pictures and Story*. New York: Dial Books for Young Readers, 1997.

Corey, Shana, with Jan Gerardi, ill. *Babe's La-La-Bye* (Jellybean Books). New York: Random House, 1999.

Davenport, Andrew, ed. *It's Tubby Bedtime* (Teletubbies). New York: Scholastic Paperbacks, 1999.

Davis, Guy, with Darren McKee, ill. *Barney Says "Night, Night."* Lyrick, 1998.

Dunbar, Joyce, with Debi Gliori, ill. *Tell Me Something Happy Before I Go to Sleep*. New York: Harcourt, Brace, 1998.

Fletcher, Rusty. *Baby is Tired*. Playskool Books, 1998.

Foreman, Michael. *Dad! I Can't Sleep!* New York: Harcourt, Brace, 1995.

Hazen, Barbara Shook, with Mary Morgan Van Royen, ill. *Where Do Bears Sleep?* New York: HarperCollins Juvenile, 1998.

Jennings, Sharon, with Mireille Levert, ill. *Sleep Tight, Mrs. Ming*. San Diego, Calif.: Annick, 1993.

Larsen, Wendy. *After Dark*. Chase, 1999.

Park, Barbara, with Denise Brunkus, ill. *Junie B. Jones Has a Monster Under Her Bed*. New York: Random House, 1997.

Pierson, Judith, with Karen Stormer Brooks, ill. *The Always Moon*. First Story, 1998.

Raschka, Christopher. *Can't Sleep*. New York: Orchard, 1995.

Roth, Carol, with Valeri Gorbachev, ill. *Little Bunny's Sleepless Night*. New York: North-South, 1999.

Dr. Seuss [Theodore Geisel]. *Dr. Seuss's Sleep Book*. New York: Random House, 1976.

Showers, Paul, with Wendy Watson, ill. *Sleep Is for Everyone* (Let's-Read-And-Find-Out Science). New York: HarperTrophy, 1997.

Simmons, Jane. *Go to Sleep, Daisy*. Boston: Little, Brown, 1999.

Stockdale, Susan. *Some Sleep Standing Up*. New York: Simon and Schuster, 1996.

Trent, John T., with Judith D. Love, ill. *There's a Duck in My Closet!* Dallas: Word Books, 1993.

Winthrop, Elizabeth, with Mary Morgan-Vanroyen, ill. *Asleep in a Heap*. New York: Holiday House, 1993.

Wood, Audrey, with Don Wood, ill. *The Napping House*. New York: Harcourt, Brace, 1994.

Zoehfeld, Kathleen, with Robbin Cuddy, ill. *Pooh's Bad Dream* (My Very First Winnie the Pooh). New York: Disney Press, 2000.

Appendix 3

Selected Scientific Publications About Infants' Sleep and Related Topics

Acebo, C., A. Sadeh, R. Seifer, O. Tzischinsky, A. R. Wolfson, A. Hafer, and M. A. Carskadon. Estimating sleep patterns with activity monitoring in children and adolescence: How many nights are necessary for reliable measures? *Sleep* 22(1999): 95–103.

Adair, R., H. Bauchner, B. Philipp, S. Levenson, and B. Zuckerman. Night waking during infancy: Role of parental presence at bedtime. *Pediatrics* 84 (1991): 500–504.

Adair, R., B. Zuckerman, H. Bauchner, B. Philipp, and S. Levenson. Reducing night waking in infancy: A primary care intervention. *Pediatrics* 89 (1992): 585–588.

Adams, L. A., and V. I. Rickert. Reducing bedtime tantrums: Comparison between positive routines and graduated extinction. *Pediatrics* 84 (1989): 756–761.

Anders, T. Infant sleep, nighttime relationships, and attachment. *Psychiatry-Interpersonal and Biological Processes* 57 (1994): 11–21.

———. Night waking in infants during the first year of life. *Pediatrics* 63 (1979): 860–864.

Anders, T. F., and L. A. Eiben. Pediatric sleep disorders: A review of the past 10 years. *Journal of the American Academy of Child and Adolescent Psychiatry* 36 (1997): 9–20.

Anders, T. F., R. Emde, and A. A. Parmelee. *A Manual of Standardized Terminology, Techniques, and Criteria for the Scoring of States of Sleep and Wakefulness in Newborn Infants.* Los Angeles: UCLA Brain Information Service, 1971.

Anders, T., B. Goodlin-Jones, and A. Sadeh. Sleep disorders. Pp. 326–338 in C. Zeanah (ed.), *Handbook of Infant Mental Health,* 2d ed. New York: Guilford, 2000.

Anders, T. F., M. Keener, T. Bowe, and B. A. Shoaff. A longitudinal study of sleep-wake patterns in infants from birth to one year. Pp. 150–169 in J. D. Call, E. Galenson, and R. L. Tyson (eds.), *Frontiers of Infant Psychiatry.* New York: Basic, 1983.

Anders, T. F., A. Sadeh, and V. Appareddy. Normal sleep in neonate and children. In R. Ferber and M. Kryger (eds.), *Principles and Practice of Sleep Medicine in the Child.* Philadelphia: W. B. Saunders, 1995.

Anders, T. F., and A. M. Sostek. The use of time-lapse video recording of sleep-wake behavior in human infants. *Psychophysiology* 13 (1976): 155–158.

Benoit, D., C. Zeanah, C. Boucher, and K. Minde. Sleep disorders in early childhood: Association with insecure maternal attachment. *Journal of the American Academy of Child and Adolescent Psychiatry* 31 (1992): 86–93.

Blair, P. S., P. J. Fleming, I. J. Smith, M. W. Platt, J. Young, P. Nadin, P. J. Berry, and J. Golding. Babies sleeping with parents: Case-control study of factors influencing the risk of the sudden infant death syndrome. *British Medical Journal* 319 (1999): 1457–1461.

Blampied, N. M, and K. G. France. A behavioral model

of infant sleep disturbance. *Journal of Applied Behavior Analysis* 26 (1993): 477–492.

Blurton-Jones, N., M. Rosetti-Ferreira, M. Farquar-Brown, and I. McDonald. The association between perinatal factors and later night waking. *Developmental Medicine and Child Neurology* 20 (1978): 427–434.

Bonnet, M. H. Effect of sleep disruption on sleep, performance, and mood. *Sleep* 8 (1985): 11–19.

Carey, W. Night waking and temperament in infancy. *Journal of Pediatrics* 84 (1974): 756–758.

Carrol, J. L., and G. M. Loughlin. Obstructive sleep apnea syndrome in infants and children: Diagnosis and management. Pp. 193–216 in R. Ferber and M. Kryger (eds.). *Principles and Practice of Sleep Medicine in the Child*. Philadelphia: W. B. Saunders, 1995.

Carroll, D. A., V. H. Denenberg, and E. B. Thoman. A comparative study of quiet sleep, active sleep, and waking in the first 2 days of life. *Developmental Psychobiology* 35 (1999): 43–48.

Coons, S. Development of sleep and wakefulness during the first 6 months of life. Pp. 17–27 in C. Guillemenault (ed.), *Sleep and Its Disorders in Children*. New York: Raven, 1987.

Davis, B. E., R. Y. Moon, H. C. Sachs, and M. C. Ottolini. Effects of sleep position on infant motor development. *Pediatrics* 102 (1998): 1135–1140.

Daws, D. *Through the Night: Helping Parents and Sleepless Infants*. London: Free Association Books, 1989.

Douglas, J., and N. Richman. *My Child Won't Sleep*. Harmondsworth: Penguin, 1984.

Durand, V. M., and J. A. Mindell. Behavioral treatment of multiple childhood sleep disorders. *Behavior Modification* 14 (1990): 37–49.

Eaton-Evans, J., and A. Dugdale. Sleep patterns of infants in the first year of life. *Archives of Disease in Child-hood* 63 (1988): 647–649.

Epstein, R., P. Herer, O. Tzischinsky, and P. Lavie. Changing from communal to familial sleep arrangement in the kibbutz: Effects on sleep quality. *Sleep* 20 (1997): 334–339.

Ferber, R. *Solve Your Child's Sleep Problem.* New York: Simon and Schuster, 1985.

Ficca, G., I. Fagioli, F. Giganti, and P. Salzarulo. Spontaneous awakenings from sleep in the first year of life. *Early Human Development* 55 (1999): 219–228.

Ficca, G., I. Fagioli, and P. Salzarulo. Sleep organization in the first year of life: Developmental trends in the quiet sleep-paradoxical sleep cycle. *Journal of Sleep Research* 9 (2000): 1–4.

France, K. G., N. M. Blampied, and P. W. Wilkinson. Treatment of infant sleep disturbance by trimeprazine in combination with extinction. *Developmental and Behavioral Pediatrics* 5 (1991): 308–314.

France, K. G., and S. M. Hudson. Behavior management of infant sleep disturbance. *Journal of Applied Behavioral Analysis* 23 (1990): 91–98.

Franco, P., A. Pardou, S. Hassid, P. Lurquin, J. Groswasser, and A. Kahn. Auditory arousal thresholds are higher when infants sleep in the prone position. *Journal of Pediatrics* 132 (1998): 240–243.

Freudigman, K. A., and E. Thoman. Infants' earliest sleep/wake organization differs as a function of delivery mode. *Developmental Psychobiology* 32 (1993): 293–303.

———. Infant sleep during the first postnatal day: An opportunity for assessment of vulnerability. *Pediatrics* 92 (1993): 373–379

Goodlin-Jones, B. L., L. A. Eiben, and T. F. Anders. Maternal well-being and sleep-wake behaviors in infants:

An intervention using maternal odor. *Infant Mental Health Journal* 18 (1997): 378–393.

Gruber, R., A. Sadeh, and A. Raviv. Instability of sleep patterns in children with attention deficit/hyperactivity disorder. *Journal of the American Academy of Child and Adolescent Psychiatry* 39 (2000): 495–501.

Guedeney, A., and L. Kreisler. Sleep disorders in the first 18 months of life: Hypothesis on the role of mother-child emotional exchanges. *Infant Mental Health Journal* 8 (1987): 307–318.

Halpern, L. F., T. F. Anders, C. G. Coll, and J. Hua. Infant temperament: Is there a relation to sleep-wake states and maternal nighttime behavior? *Infant Behavior and Development* 17 (1994): 255–263.

Hoppenbrouwers, T. Sleep in infants. Pp. 1–15 in C. Guillemenault (ed.), *Sleep and Its Disorders in Children*. New York: Raven, 1987.

Ingersoll, E. W., and E. B. Thoman. Sleep/wake states of preterm infants: Stability, developmental change, diurnal variation, and relation with caregiving activity. *Child Development* 70 (1999): 1–10.

Jacklin C., M. Snow, M. Gahart, and E. Maccoby. Sleep pattern development from 6 through 33 months. *Journal of Pediatric Psychology* 5 (1980): 295–303.

Johnson, M. Infant and toddler sleep: A telephone survey of parents in one community. *Journal of Developmental and Behavioral Pediatrics* 12 (1991): 108–114.

Jones, D. P. H., and C. M. Verduyn. Behavioural management of sleep problems. *Archives of Diseases in Childhood* 58 (1983): 442–444.

Kahn, A., M. Mozin, E. Rebuffat, M. Sottiaux, and M. F. Muller. Milk intolerance in children with persistent sleeplessness: A prospective double-blind crossover evaluation. *Pediatrics* 84 (1989): 595–603.

Kahn, A., E. Rebuffat, M. Sottiaux, D. Dufour, S. Cadranel, and F. Reiterer. Arousals induced by proximal esophageal reflux in infants. *Sleep* 14 (1991): 39–42.

Kateria, S., M. Swanson, and G. Trevarthin. Persistence of sleep disturbances in preschool children. *Journal of Pediatrics* 110 (1987): 642–646.

Kattwinkel, J., J. S. Brooks, M. E. Keenen, and M. Malloy. Changing concepts of sudden infant death syndrome: Implications for infant sleeping environment and sleep position. *Pediatrics* 105 (2000): 650–656.

Keefe, M. Comparison of neonatal nighttime sleep-wake patterns in nursery versus rooming-in environments. *Nursery Research* 36 (1987): 140–144.

Keener, M., C. Zeanah, and T. Anders. Infant temperament, sleep organization, and nighttime parental intervention. *Pediatrics* 81 (1988): 762–771.

Lavie, P., O. Tzischinsky, and A. Sadeh. Sleep and its disorders during the first decade. Pp. 268–285 in D. Bar Tal and A. Klingman (eds.), *Selected Psychological Issues in Education*. Jerusalem: Ministry of Education, 1990 (Hebrew).

Lawton, C., K. G. France, and N. M. Blampied. Treatment of infant sleep disturbance by graduated extinction. *Child and Family Behavior Therapy* 13 (1991): 39–56.

Lozoff, B., A. W. Wolf, and N. S. Davis. Cosleeping in urban families with young children in the United States. *Pediatrics* 74 (1984): 171–182.

———. Sleep problems seen in pediatric practice. *Pediatrics* 75 (1985): 477–483.

Macknin, M., S. Medendorp, and M. Maier. Infant sleep and bedtime cereal. *American Journal of Diseases of Children* 143 (1989): 1066–1068.

Macknin, M. L., M. Piedmonte, J. Jacobs, and C. Skibinski. Symptoms associated with infant teething: A prospective study. *Pediatrics* 105 (2000): 747–752.

McGarr, R. J., and M. F. Hovell. In search of the sandman: Shaping an infant to sleep. *Education and Treatment of Children* 3 (1980): 173–182.

McKenna, J. J., E. B. Thoman, T. F. Anders, A. Sadeh, V. L. Schechterman, and S. F. Glotzbach. Infant-parent cosleeping in an evolutionary perspective: Implications for understanding infant sleep development and the sudden infant death syndrome. *Sleep* 16 (1993): 263–282.

Messer, D. J., L. Lauder, and S. Humphery. The effectiveness of group therapy in treating children's sleeping problems. *Child: Care, Health, and Development* 20 (1994): 267–277.

Minard, K. L., K. Freudigman, and E. B. Thoman. Sleep rhythmicity in infants: Index of stress or maturation. *Behavioural Processes* 47 (1999): 189–203.

Minde, K., A. Faucon, and S. Falkner. Sleep problems in toddlers: Effects of treatment on their daytime behavior. *Journal of the American Academy of Child and Adolescent Psychiatry* 33 (1994): 1114–1121.

Mindell, J. A. Empirically supported treatments in pediatric psychology: Bedtime refusal and night wakings in young children. *Journal of Pediatric Psychology* 24 (1999): 465–481.

Moore, M. Disturbed attachment in children: A factor in sleep disturbance, altered dream production, and immune dysfunction. *Journal of Child Psychotherapy* 15 (1989): 99–111.

Moore, T., and L. Ucko. Night waking in early infancy, part 1. *Archives of Disease in Childhood* 32 (1957): 333–342.

Morrell, J. M. B. The role of maternal cognitions in infant sleep problems as assessed by a new instrument, the maternal cognitions about infant sleep questionnaire. *Journal of Child Psychology and Psychiatry and Allied Disciplines* 40 (1999): 247–258.

Nagera, H. Sleep and its disturbances approached developmentally. *Psychoanalytic Study of the Child* 21 (1966): 393–447.

Nakamura, S., M. Wind, and M. A. Danello. Review of hazards associated with children placed in adult beds. *Archives of Pediatrics and Adolescent Medicine* 153 (1999): 1019–1023.

Novosad, C., K. Freudigman, and E. B. Thoman. Sleep patterns in newborns and temperament at eight months: A preliminary study. *Journal of Developmental and Behavioral Pediatrics* 20 (1999): 99–105.

Ophir-Cohen, M., R. Epstein, O. Tzischinsky, E. Tirosh, and P. Lavie. Sleep patterns of children sleeping in residential care, in Kibbutz dormitories and at home: A comparative study. *Sleep* 16 (1993): 428–432.

Owens, J. L., K. G. France, and L. Wiggs. Behavioural and cognitive-behavioural interventions for sleep disorders in infants and children: A review. *Sleep Medicine Reviews* 3 (1999): 281–302.

Paret, I. Night waking and its relationship to mother-infant interaction in nine-month-old infants. Pp. 171–177 in J. Call, E. Galenson, and R. Tyson (eds.), *Frontiers of Infant Psychiatry*. New York: Basic, 1983.

Pillar, G., A. Sadeh, N. Peled, R. Peled, and P. Lavie. Insomnia in infants and children: Causes, significance, diagnosis, and treatment. *Harefua* (Israel Journal of Medicine) 130 (1996): 255–259 (Hebrew).

Pinilla, T., and L. L. Birch. Help me make it through the night: Behavioral entrainment of breast-fed infants' sleep patterns. *Pediatrics* 91 (1993): 436–444.

Ramchandani, P., L. Wiggs, V. Webb, and G. Stores. A systematic review of treatments for settling problems and night waking in young children. *British Medical Journal* 320 (2000): 209–213.

Reid, M. J., A. L. Walter, and S. G. O'Leary. Treatment of young children's bedtime refusal and nighttime wakings: A comparison of "standard" and graduated ignoring procedures. *Journal of Abnormal Child Psychology* 27 (1999): 5–16.

Richman, N. A community survey of characteristics of one- to two-year-olds with sleep disruptions. *Journal of the American Academy of Child Psychiatry* 20 (1981): 281–291.

Richman, N., J. Douglas, H. Hunt, R. Landsdown, and R. Levere. Behavioral methods in the treatment of sleep disorders: A pilot study. *Journal of Child Psychology and Psychiatry* 26 (1985): 581–590.

Rickert, V. I., and C. M. Johnson. Reducing nocturnal awakening and crying episodes in infants and young children: A comparison between scheduled awakening and systematic ignoring. *Pediatrics* 81 (1988): 203–212.

Sadeh, A. Actigraphic home monitoring of sleep disturbed infants: Comparison to controls and assessment of intervention. Pp. 469–470 in J. Horne (ed.), *Sleep '90*. Bochum: Pontenagel, 1990.

———. Assessment of intervention for infant night waking: Parental reports and activity-based home monitoring. *Journal of Consulting and Clinical Psychology* 62 (1994): 63–98.

———. Evaluating night-wakings in sleep-disturbed infants: A methodological study of parental reports and actigraphy. *Sleep* 19 (1996): 757–762.

———. Melatonin and sleep in infants: A preliminary study. *Sleep* 20 (1997): 185–191.

———. Maturation of normal sleep patterns from childhood through adolescence. Pp. 63–78 in G. M. Loughlin, J. L. Carroll, and C. L. Marcus (eds.), *Sleep and Breathing in Children: A Developmental Approach*. New York: Marcel Dekker, 2000.

————. Sleep disorders in childhood: Scientific update. *Pediatric Update* 15 (1996): 11–13 (Hebrew).

————. Stress, trauma, and sleep in children. In E. R. Dahl (ed.), *Child and Adolescent Psychiatric Clinics of North America* 5 (1996): 685–700.

Sadeh, A., Acebo, C., Seifer, R., Aytur, S., and Carskadon, M. A. Activity-based assessment of sleep-wake patterns during the first year of life. *Infant Behavior and Development* 18 (1995): 329–337.

Sadeh, A., and T. F. Anders. Sleep Disorders. Pp. 305–316 in C. H. Zeanah (ed.), *Handbook of Infant Mental Health*. New York: Guilford, 1993.

————. Infant sleep problems: Origins, assessment, intervention. *Infant Mental Health Journal* 14 (1993): 17–34.

Sadeh, A., I. Dark, and B. R. Vohr. Newborns' sleep-wake patterns: The role of maternal, delivery, and infant factors. *Early Human Development* 44 (1996): 113–126.

Sadeh, A., and R. Gruber. Sleep Disorders. Pp. 629–653 in A. S. Bellack and M. Hersen (eds.), *Comprehensive Clinical Psychology*. New York: Pergamon, 1998.

Sadeh, A., P. Hauri, D. Kripke, and P. Lavie. The role of actigraphy in sleep medicine. *Sleep* 18 (1995): 288–302.

Sadeh, A., P. Lavie, and A. Scher. Maternal perceptions of temperament of sleep-disturbed toddlers. *Early Education and Development* 5 (1994): 311–322.

Sadeh, A., P. Lavie, A. Scher, E. Tirosh, and R. Epstein. Actigraphic home-monitoring of sleep-disturbed and control infants and young children: A new method for pediatric assessment of sleep-wake patterns. *Pediatrics* 87 (1991): 494–499.

Sadeh, A., A. Raviv, and R. Gruber. Sleep patterns and

sleep disruptions in school-age children. *Developmental Psychology* 36 (2000): 291–301.

Salzarulo, P., and A. Chevalier. Sleep problems in children and their relationships with early disturbances of the waking-sleeping rhythms. *Sleep* 6 (1983): 47–51.

Schacter, F., M. Fuchs, P. Bijur, and R. Stone. Cosleeping and sleep problems in Hispanic American urban young children. *Pediatrics* 84 (1989): 522–530.

Schaefer, C. Night waking and temperament in early childhood. *Psychological Report* 67 (1990): 192–194.

Scher, A., and O. Blumberg. Night waking among 1-year olds: A study of maternal separation anxiety. *Child Care, Health, and Development* 25 (1999): 323–334.

Scher, A., R. Epstein, A. Sadeh, E. Tirosh, and P. Lavie. Toddlers' sleep and temperament: Reporting bias or valid link? A research note. *Journal of Child Psychology and Child Psychiatry* 33 (1992): 1249–1254.

Scher, A., E. Tirosh, M. Jaffe, L. Rubin, A. Sadeh, and P. Lavie. Sleep patterns of infants and young children in Israel. *International Journal of Behavioral Development* 18 (1995): 701–711.

Scher, A., E. Tirosh, and P. Lavie. The relationship between sleep and temperament revisited: Evidence for 12-month-olds. A research note. *Journal of Child Psychology and Psychiatry and Allied Disciplines* 39 (1998): 785–788.

Scott, G., and M. Richards. Night waking in infants: Effects of providing advice and support for parents. *Journal of Child Psychology and Psychiatry* 31 (1990): 551–567.

Seifer, R., A. J. Sameroff, S. Dickstein, L. C. Hayden, and M. Schiller. Parental psychopathology and sleep variation in children. In E. R. Dahl (ed), *Child and Adolescent Psychiatric Clinics of North America* 5 (1996): 715–727.

Seymour, F. W., P. Brock, M. During, and G. Pole. Reducing sleep disruptions in young children: Evaluation of therapist-guided and written information approaches. A brief report. *Journal of Child Psychiatry* 30 (1989): 913–918.

Simonds, J., and H. Parraga. Sleep behaviors and disorders in children and adolescents evaluated at psychiatric clinics. *Developmental and Behavioral Pediatrics* 5 (1984): 6–10.

Thoman, E. B. Morningness and eveningness: Issues for study of the early ontogeny of these circadian rhythms. *Human Development* 42 (1999): 206–212.

———. Sleep and wake behaviors in the neonates: Consistencies and consequences. *Merrill-Palmer Quarterly* 21 (1975): 295–314.

Thoman, E. B., K. Hammond, G. Affleck, and H. N. Desilva. The breathing bear with preterm infants: Effects on sleep, respiration, and affect. *Infant Mental Health Journal* 16 (1995): 160–168.

Thoman, E. B., E. W. Ingersoll, and C. Acebo. Premature infants seek rhythmic stimulation, and the experience facilitates neurobehavioral development. *Developmental and Behavioral Pediatrics* 12 (1991): 11–18.

Thoman, E. B., and M. P. Whitney. Sleep states in infants monitored at home: Individual differences, developmental trends, and origins of diurnal cyclicity. *Infant Behavior and Development* 12 (1989): 59–75.

Tirosh, E., A. Scher, A. Sadeh, M. Jaffe, and P. Lavie. Sleep characteristics of asthmatics in the first four years of life: A comparative study. *Archives of Disease in Childhood* 68 (1993): 481–483.

Tirosh, E., A. Scher, A. Sadeh, M. Jaffe, A. Rubin, and P. Lavie. The effects of illness on sleep behaviour in infants. *European Journal of Pediatrics* 152 (1992): 15–17.

Toselli, M., P. Farneti, and P. Salzarulo. Maternal representation and care of infant sleep. *Early Development and Parenting* 7 (1998): 73–78.

Van Tassel, E. B. The relative influence of child and environmental characteristics on sleep disturbances in the first and second years of life. *Developmental and Behavioral Pediatrics* 6 (1985): 81–86.

Weissbluth, M. Modification of sleep schedule with reduction of night waking: A case report. *Sleep* 5 (1982): 262–266.

Weissbluth, M., A. Davis, and J. Poucher. Night waking in 4- to 8-month-old infants. *Journal of Pediatrics* 104 (1984): 477–480.

Wiggs, L., and G. Stores. Behavioural treatment for sleep problems in children with severe learning disabilities and challenging daytime behaviour: Effect on sleep patterns of mother and child. *Journal of Sleep Research* 7 (1998): 119–126.

Wolf, A. W., and B. Lozoff. Object attachment, thumbsucking, and the passage to sleep. *Journal of the American Academy of Child and Adolescent Psychiatry* 28 (1989): 287–292.

Wolfson, A., P. Lacks, and A. Futterman. Effects of parent training on infant sleeping patterns, parents' stress, and perceived parental competence. *Journal of Consulting and Clinical Psychology* 60 (1992): 41–48.

Wright, P., H. Macleod, and M. Cooper. Waking at night: The effect of early feeding. *Child: Care, Health, and Development* 9 (1983): 309–319.

Zuckerman, B., J. Stevenson, and V. Baily. Sleep problems in early childhood: Predictive factors and behavioral correlates. *Pediatrics* 80 (1987): 664–671.

Index

Page numbers in **bold** type refer to tables or figures.

Index

Sher, Anat, 75, 100

sibling relationships, 65, 79–80, 153

SIDS (sudden infant death syndrome). *See* sudden infant death syndrome (SIDS)

sleep, active: cycles (biological clock), 10–11; definition of, 11–12; importance of studying, 8–9; quiet, 9–10, 11, 22–23, **23**; role of, 3–6; stages of, 13, 174, 175. *See also* dream-sleep; observation methods

sleep, amount of: birth to seven years old, **19**; and mental function, 3–4, 52–53; for newborns, 18–20, 25; newborns/one-year olds, comparison of, **20**; and physical growth, 41–44; and sleep phenomena, 106, 109

sleep apnea, 117–121; and physical growth, 42, 44; and sudden infant death syndrome, 124; symptoms of, 118–119; treatment of, 119–120

sleep consolidation, 26, 30, 31–33. *See also* newborn sleep

sleep deprivation, and mental function, 3–4, 52–53

sleep diaries, 16–17, 178, 179, 180

sleep patterns, formation of. *See* newborn sleep

sleep position, 115, 124

sleep talking, 108–109

sleepwalking, 108–109

sleep watches: as an observation tool, 15, **15**, **16**, 178; as transitional object, 75–76, 143

snoring, 118

soothing techniques, 68–77, **74**; in behavior therapy, 142–143; learned from parents, 68–69; as a sign of independence, 69–70; transitional objects as, 70–71, 73, 74, 75–76, 95; transitional phenomena as, 70, 71–75, 76–77, 95

stomach pain (colic), 115

stormy sleep. *See* dream-sleep

stress, 54–60; causes of, in babies, 57; defined, 56; and falling asleep, 94–95; and night terrors, 106; of parents, and child's response to, 54–56; Persian Gulf War study, 58–60; response patterns to, 60; and self-soothing, 69; in sleep laboratories, 57–58; and sleep phenomena, 106, 109. *See also* separation anxiety

substance abuse, 114

sudden infant death syndrome (SIDS), 122–127; and cosleeping, 81; loss, repercus-